The Logic of Evangelism

The Logic of Evangelism

Revisited

EDITED BY

Michael J. Gehring,
Andrew D. Kinsey,
Vaughn W. Baker

FOREWORD BY *William B. Lawrence*
AFTERWORD BY *William J. Abraham*

PICKWICK *Publications* · Eugene, Oregon

THE LOGIC OF EVANGELISM
Revisited

Pickwick Publications
An Imprint of Wipf and Stock Publishers
199 W. 8th Ave., Suite 3
Eugene, OR 97401

www.wipfandstock.com

PAPERBACK ISBN: 978-1-5326-0456-0
HARDCOVER ISBN: 978-1-5326-0458-4
EBOOK ISBN: 978-1-5326-0457-7

Cataloguing-in-Publication data:

Names: Gehring, Michael J., editor. | Kinsey, Andrew D., editor. | Baker, Vaughan Willard, editor. | Lawrence, William B. (William Benjamin), foreword. | Abraham, William J. (William James), afterword.

Title: The logic of evangelism : revisited / edited by Michael J. Gehring, Andrew D. Kinsey, and Vaughn W. Baker; foreword by William B. Lawrence; afterword.

Description: Eugene, OR: Pickwick Publications, 2019 | Series: if applicable | Includes bibliographical references and index.

Identifiers: ISBN 978-1-5326-0456-0 (paperback) | ISBN 978-1-5326-0458-4 (hardcover) | ISBN 978-1-5326-0457-7 (ebook)

Subjects: LCSH: Evangelistic work. | Abraham, William J. (William James), 1947-— Criticism and interpretation.

Classification: BV3790 .L70 2019 (print) | BV3790 .L70 (ebook)

Manufactured in the U.S.A.   February 4, 2019

Contents

Contents

Foreword

IT IS QUITE POSSIBLE that if we were to ask, "What is the most *powerful* program in the ministries of the church?" and, "What is the most *problematic* program in the ministries of the church?" the answer to both questions might be the same: *evangelism.*

The *power* of evangelism is its Christological mandate. In the Great Commission from the risen Lord—whether one reads it in Matthew 28, John 21, or Acts 1—the good news of Jesus Christ is an empowering gift offered to others. We have authority from the Lord to evangelize with many methods: in preaching, teaching, and baptizing, as Jesus describes it through Matthew; in caring for all of God's children with everything from food to forgiveness, as Jesus describes it through John; and in reaching the ends of the earth, as Jesus communicates before the Ascension in Acts.

The *problem* with evangelism is the way we have packaged it. Sometimes in the history of the church, we have turned it into mere tactics for church growth, settling for statistical satisfactions about the number of churches we have started or the number of members we have recruited. Sometimes in the history of the church, we have confused it with reviving the enthusiasm of current members, and we have substituted revivalism for a real sharing of the good news with those who remain unreached. And sometimes in the history of the church, we have weaponized it; assuming that if we could just impose our own form of "religion" upon others in the world through political control—or even warfare—we would be winning souls for Christ.

In every generation, Christians have to rediscover and reclaim the power of the good news without replicating the problems that have bedeviled us. We must, as Saint Paul said in the letter to the Romans, not be ashamed of the gospel. At the same time, we must not do shameful things in the name of the gospel. Evangelism is serious spiritual work in the name of Christ. It deserves both the deepest dedication of our souls and the highest intellectual standards of our minds. Among the great endeavors to take evangelism seriously in recent years has been The Polycarp Community at Perkins School of Theology.

For several decades, Perkins has had a Missional Center that devoted specific attention to evangelism. Under a succession of directors, it has launched an array of projects. The Center has trained laity through certificate programs in ministries of evangelism. It has linked interest in communal life under a neo-monastic rule with community outreach. It forged a respectful connection between the evangelistic mission of the church and the reconciling mission of the church with interfaith communities. Today, the Center for Evangelism and Missional Church Studies at Perkins School of Theology continues to fulfill its purposes through substantive, practical initiatives in academic and ecclesiastical settings.

One serious effort that has been underway for many years involves convening groups of evangelism scholars with global vision and respect for the power of the Holy Spirit in the mission of evangelization. It came into being with the formation of "The Polycarp Community."

Under the auspices of Professor William J. Abraham, who began his work on the Perkins faculty as a professor of evangelism and who has been the Albert Cook Outler Professor of Wesley Studies for decades, an international gathering of academic leaders in the field of evangelism has dedicated itself to reclaiming the power of evangelism for both academic and ministerial purposes.

Within The Polycarp Community, senior scholars who are engaged in research on evangelism, pastors with terminal degrees who engage in the work of evangelism, and graduate students who are writing dissertations in various aspects of evangelism create Christian conferencing around the issues that are vital to faithful evangelistic mission.

The Polycarp Community has a fully orbed program in Christians' obligation to the mission of the church. Dr. Abraham has noted that Christian mission includes the themes of justice, healthy local communities, healthy nations, care of the poor, and care of the environment. Evangelism, he insists, is located within that broader mission of Christianity. It is not only about proclamation *of* the gospel but also about nurturing disciples *in* the gospel so that God's people can be transformed *with* the gospel.

Perhaps the very name of this endeavor is a sign of its feistiness. By calling those who participate in this project "The Polycarp Community," we can sense its connection to the deep history, durable theology, diverse ethnicity, and dedicated spirituality of the evangelizing that the church has been called to do. Polycarp was one of the Christians martyred in the second century. He belonged to the generation that followed the era of the apostles who had been personal witnesses to the life of Christ on earth and who shared the story in the earliest tasks of evangelism. He helped form the teachings of the church before the adoption of formal creeds. He also became the Bishop of Smyrna, which is now the modern city of Izmir in Turkey, not far from the place where Europe and Asia meet, in the midst of the place where most of the important early Christian history occurred and at the crossroads of great religions today. He committed to writing his views on teaching and practicing the faith, thus leaving a record of the foundations of faith for Christians in every millennium to come. For The Polycarp Community, the work of evangelism is not to be separated from the history, the theology, and the liturgy of Christianity.

These reflections of those who participate in The Polycarp Community continue that dedication. They are the scholars of evangelism and the practitioners of leadership in the church's ministries of evangelism. Like Polycarp in his era, they witness in this age so that there will be witnesses in the age to come.

William B. Lawrence

Acknowledgments

We want to thank the contributors of this volume for the following essays recognizing William J. Abraham's *The Logic of Evangelism*. We are grateful for their efforts to probe more deeply into a book that has become a classic in the field of evangelism. It is a privilege to assemble the insights of both teachers and practitioners in the ministry and field of evangelism. The content they share represents a cross-section of views and offers the deep appreciation of those who have worked with and learned from Abraham over the years. Their work seeks to honor him as well as continue the conversation about the church's overall mission of evangelism. Special thanks must go to Dean William B. Lawrence, who wrote the Foreword, and, of course, to Professor Abraham for the Afterword.

Learning that evangelism is a field of research and study in and of itself has shifted the focus of evangelism and introduced a whole network of associations now seeking renewal in the church. Abraham's mark has been left. *The Logic of Evangelism* has ushered in a new era.

This volume is one small gesture toward recognizing the significant impact of Abraham in the field of evangelism and with continuing the trajectory of that work.

Andrew D. Kinsey
Michael J. Gehring
Vaughn W. Baker

Chapter One

The Theory and Practice of Evangelism

Philip Meadows

I WAS FIRST INTRODUCED to *The Logic of Evangelism* in the summer of 1994 while on a mission trip to Bulgaria.[1] It was not long after the collapse of Communism, and the church was beginning to enjoy a new season of religious freedom. The pastor of the Methodist Church in Sophia was an American missionary who turned out to be a kindred spirit as we celebrated the work of God in Bulgaria and lamented the failure of evangelistic zeal in the mainline denominations back home. He asked if I had heard of William J. Abraham, as *The Logic of Evangelism* had impacted his own calling and ministry. He was excited that Abraham's work not only provided an effective vision for evangelism but also helped to give an intellectual respectability to the subject and greater confidence to evangelical Christians in seminary education. Shortly after returning home, I sat in my study, reading the book. A few years later, I stood in a classroom quoting from it as a seminary professor. More than twenty years later, it is still on my required or recommended reading list for classes in the theology of evangelism.

The original subtitle of *The Logic of Evangelism* was "a significant contribution to the theory and practice of evangelism." As a teacher of missiology and evangelism, however, I am acutely aware of the gap that exists between theory and practice. Recognizing the weakness in our practice can stimulate the need for better academic reflection, and improvements in our theory can certainly stimulate a fresh interest in evangelistic mission. It is

---

1. See Abraham, *Logic of Evangelism*.

also equally possible to have all the theory and none of the practice. In what follows, I will review the central arguments of *The Logic of Evangelism*, and follow with a few concerns of Abraham's overall project.

The Evangelism Gap

Thanks to the efforts of Abraham and others, the contemporary church has never been supplied with better theologies, deeper wisdom, or richer teaching and training in evangelism than at present. Given the general state of church decline in the West, we have never had greater motivation to put these things into practice! However, evidence suggests this situation is not having the desired impact on the evangelistic witness of the church—especially in the trenches.[2] The reasons are complex, and we will turn to *The Logic of Evangelism* to help us expose some of them.

Evangelism in Theory

Abraham stated his intention to write a book that makes a case for "taking evangelism radically seriously as a topic of theological enquiry" and "to delineate the contours of an ongoing research program that could well constitute the beginnings of a new field within the discipline of theology."[3] He sets out to accomplish this task by pursuing three subsidiary aims: first, "to conceive of evangelism as initiation into the kingdom of God"; second, to "demonstrate the necessity for an interdisciplinary approach to the theory and practice of evangelism"; and, third, that this might "provoke or inspire other scholars either to provide a better way of pursuing critical reflection on evangelism," or to take up and improve on his own argument.[4]

It is fair to say that the academic aspirations of *The Logic of Evangelism* have been more than fully realized and most certainly within the broad Wesleyan tradition to which Abraham belongs. There is now a substantial body of work on the theology and practice of evangelism from a variety of perspectives and disciplines, some of which critically and creatively extend the arguments in the book. Much of this work has been influenced

2. For empirical research on the failure of Christians to engage in the basic evangelistic practice of faith sharing, see: "Churchgoers Believe in Sharing Faith," and "Is Evangelism Going Out of Style?"

3. Abraham, *Logic of Evangelism*, 1–2.

4. Abraham, *Logic of Evangelism*, 15.

by developments in the field of missiology, which have emphasized the now-and-not-yet kingdom of God as an eschatological framework for understanding the role of evangelism. Professional guilds in the field of evangelization studies have been also strengthened,[5] and professorships in evangelism have become well established.[6]

Evangelism in Practice

In his Preface to *The Logic of Evangelism*, Andrew Walker of King's College in London writes, "Billy Abraham is a pastor and an evangelist as well as an academic."[7] Walker's observation has been my personal experience as well, and it shines through the book in both its style and content. Abraham's overarching aspiration for the book is to stimulate a fresh confidence in the practice of evangelism at a time of crisis and opportunity in the church. From the perspective of 1989, he predicted that there would be "a very significant outburst of evangelism as the church heads toward a new century" and that the church would come to acknowledge that "the Western world needs to be evangelized afresh." In the midst of deepening secularization, he observed a growing consensus that "evangelism must become a top priority for the modern church."[8]

Let me make some observations from my own context in the United Kingdom. In line with Abraham's prediction, the 1990s were formally designated a Decade of Evangelism, but they could hardly be assessed as a "significant 'outburst' of evangelistic fervor."[9] The church pushed for church planting, developing mission-shaped churches, and ecumenical initiatives like Fresh Expressions.[10] Now, the necessity of mission, evangelism, and making disciples has become a well-established priority in the rhetoric and polity of many mainline denominations.[11] Although there are mixed signs

5. A good example is the Academy for Evangelism in Theological Education, which was founded in 1973.

6. See, for example, the strategic initiative by the Foundation for Evangelism in establishing E. Stanley Jones professorships of evangelism in Methodist-related seminaries and universities (Gunter, "E. Stanley Jones Professors").

7. Abraham, *Logic of Evangelism*, viii.

8. Abraham, *Logic of Evangelism*, 12.

9. See, for example, Francis and Roberts, "Growth or Decline in the Church," 67–81, and Field, "Assessing the Decade of Evangelism."

10. This history is summarized in Church of England, *Mission-Shaped Church*.

11. The Reform & Renewal group in the Church of England has a key goal to

of growth and decline, the overarching trend in church membership and attendance reveals a state of severe attrition. For example, the Church of England declined by around 100,000 members in 2005–2015,[12] and the Methodist Church in Great Britain lost around a third of its total membership in approximately the same period.[13] There is little evidence that this trend will change anytime soon. If anything, the renewed concern for evangelism may have exposed an underlying lack of spiritual vitality, confidence in the gospel, and ability to share faith with non-Christians. During his inaugural address as President of the British Methodist Conference in 2015, the Rev. Steven Wild urged the denomination to "take God seriously" in the task of evangelism. He urged them "to put mission on the agenda and give our churches an aim to win a person for Christ." In other words, within the coming year, the challenge was simply "to bring one person to faith—to make one new member." It is telling that he had to remind them, "It is not impossible!"[14]

Re-Evangelizing the Church

In assessing *The Logic of Evangelism*, it seems to me that it begins and ends with an underlying spiritual conviction. Without the experiential reality of abiding in the kingdom of God and the power of the Holy Spirit to transform our lives, there can be no authentic evangelism. If the church is not alive to God, it will lack evangelistic zeal for the least and the lost as well as the capacity to make true converts or disciples. For Abraham, the "logic of evangelism" is closely coupled to the need for renewal, and he observes that the church itself may need to be evangelized afresh.[15] A passion for evangelism is not an optional extra for the church but fundamental to its very nature: "If the church does not evangelize, it has forfeited the right to be called apostolic, and apostolicity is an ineradicable mark of the church's

---

"facilitate the growth of the church in numbers and depth of discipleship" (Church of England, "Renewal & Reform"). The Methodist Church in Great Britain summarizes its calling "to respond to the gospel of God's love in Christ and to live out its discipleship in worship and mission" (Methodist Church, "Views of the Church").

12. See Church of England, "Statistics for Mission 2015," 11.

13. See, for example, Methodist Church, "Statistics for Mission 2014."

14. See Methodist Church, "Bring One Person to Faith."

15. Abraham, *Logic of Evangelism*, 12–13. See also Abraham, *Logic of Renewal*.

identity."[16] Given the urgency of the present task, however, the church may not have the luxury of time to get its own house in order before reaching out to others. Rather, with a better vision of what evangelism entails, we are urged to venture out in fear and trembling and to discover that "in evangelizing, the church itself is re-evangelized."[17]

The Logic of Initiation

Abraham writes with the motivation of an evangelist. His aim is to win the reader to a better vision of the gospel as good news of the reign of God and what it means to live as a faithful citizen in God's kingdom. Having captivated our minds and hearts to this vision, he invites then to repent of our old ways and believe that evangelism is a much more ordinary, yet demanding set of activities than we assumed.

In particular, we are to repent of the mistakes inherited from the traditional models of proclamation and church growth. Every non-evangelist breathes a sigh of relief as the distasteful images of street preaching, crusading, and televangelism are exposed as flawed and inadequate approaches to spreading the gospel. Abraham confirms our worst suspicions that such para-church approaches to evangelism have focused on making converts rather than disciples. All those who have been burned out by the technocratic mindset of the church growth school take little persuading that searching for the one-best-way to organize the church for evangelistic mission is a dangerous illusion. Marketing and programmatic approaches to evangelism have focused on attracting seekers but have ended up making consumers of religion rather than citizens and agents of the kingdom. Filling churches with stunted converts and religious consumers cannot be the goal of evangelism.

The Goal of Evangelism

Freed from the burden of mistaken approaches, Abraham then encourages us to re-imagine the "logic of evangelism" as a means to the end of living under the reign of God. Abraham puts it this way: "We can best improve our thinking on evangelism by conceiving of it as that set of intentional

---

16. Abraham, *Logic of Evangelism*, 167.

17. Abraham, *Logic of Evangelism*, 113, 170.

activities which is governed by the goal of initiating people into the kingdom of God for the first time."[18] We can accomplish these "intentional activities" through participation in the community and ministry of the church where "life-together" embodies the real presence of the kingdom and equips people for a journey of conversion and holistic formation.

Abraham describes evangelism as a "polymorphous activity" that includes proclamation, basic instruction in the faith, equipping with spiritual disciplines, nurturing in small groups, and releasing spiritual gifts. These activities conform to the logic of evangelism, as "part of a process that is governed by the goal of initiating people into the kingdom of God."[19] This process facilitates a journey of faith in which one makes a personal decision to live under the reign of God, moving to baptism or confirmation. Although the experiences associated with evangelical conversion are an intentional outcome of evangelism as initiation into the kingdom of God, Abraham reconnects evangelism to the bigger task of making authentic disciples.

The Means of Evangelism

Describing evangelism as a polymorphous activity also provides a way for conceiving how any practice in the church has the potential to become evangelistic in character. Abraham identifies three essential ingredients in this ministry of evangelism.[20]

First, Abraham argues for the priority of corporate worship, which immerses people in the real presence of God, as a Spirit-filled expression of life in the kingdom. Ultimately, evangelism is a spiritual issue. It should proceed from joyful witness to the first-hand experience of living under the reign of God in the realities of daily life. This witness should lead to the incorporation of others into a church that bears a numinous witness to the presence of their first-love. Where the church merely talks or sings about the Spirit—and does not actually know the Spirit in experience—the church needs to remedy the problem. In recent years, for example, this theme has gained wide scholarly attention from many different traditions.

18. Abraham, *Logic of Evangelism*, 95. For a critique of Abraham's thesis in terms of the goal of evangelism, see Yeich, "Christian Perfection," 178, 188.

19. Abraham, *Logic of Evangelism*, 104.

20. See Abraham, *Logic of Evangelism*, 164–84.

These traditions emphasize the evangelistic nature of worship itself as well as the potential for worship to form our everyday witness.[21]

The second essential ingredient is proclamation. By this, Abraham includes all forms of speech that are motivated by the aim of initiating people into the kingdom of God. Preaching in church and personal conversation over coffee become evangelistic when the witness of the Spirit in the believer connects with the prevenient work of the Spirit in the other and there is an invitation to respond. The evangelist is someone gifted in the art of proclamation. Taking the gospel of the kingdom as a starting point, there has been much scholarly interest in re-examining the centrality of proclamation to the meaning of evangelism, not least from Jesus himself. Such research has involved re-connecting the task of proclamation to the ministry of the church itself, both gathered and scattered.[22]

Third, and perhaps most crucial for Abraham's proposal, is the need for catechesis in the intellectual, moral, and spiritual dimensions of a life made fit for the kingdom of God. Abraham suggests a recovery and adaptation of the catechumenate found in the early church, whereby church aims at the conversion of persons to the way of Jesus in mind, heart, and life. The decision to become a catechumen is the outcome of proclamation, while effective proclamation is the overflow of an authentically worshipful life, and life-transforming worship is the matrix for authentically evangelistic catechesis. In the increasingly post-Christendom culture of the West, this intuition has coincided with a rise of scholarly interest in the pre-Christendom emphasis on catechesis and making disciples.[23]

The Agents of Evangelism

Just as we cannot reduce evangelism to a single activity, so we cannot reduce it to a "solo performance." First, evangelism is primarily the work of the triune God: in all God has done for us in Christ to save us from our sins, and all that God does in us through the Spirit to transform our lives

---

21. For approaches that seek to avoid the instrumentalization of worship, see Senn, *Witness of the Worshipping Community*; Morgenthaler, *Worship Evangelism*; Dawn, *Reaching Out Without Dumbing Down*; and Kreider and Kreider, *Worship and Mission*.

22. See, for example, Klaiber, *Call and Response*, and Arias, *Announcing the Reign of God*. Jack Jackson has argued for returning to the simple definition of evangelism as the complex and subtle art of proclamation or spiritual conversation (in multiple contexts) that moves people through the whole way of salvation. See Jackson, *Offering Christ*.

23. See, for example, Kreider, *Change of Conversion*, and Webber, *Journey to Jesus*.

and empower our witness in the world.[24] Second, evangelism is the work of the church, which embodies the reality of the kingdom in its life together, providing visible evidence and tangible encounter with the reign of God. Third, evangelism is the work of the evangelist, whose task is to proclaim the gospel and to ensure those who respond are properly catechized in the life and ways of the kingdom. Finally, evangelism is the work of the evangelized themselves, whose responsibility is to wrestle with the truth of the gospel and to cooperate with the Spirit in the process of catechesis as those actively seeking the kingdom of God.[25]

We might think of this approach to evangelism, along with the evangelistic orientation of its constituent activities and agents, as a "means of grace." It is not merely that God is the primary agent, but that the entire evangelistic enterprise aims at a goal only accomplished by God's grace. The agencies of church, evangelist, and evangelized are responding to—and acting in cooperation with—the missional movements of the Holy Spirit: to initiate people into the kingdom of God. In short, Abraham is concerned to establish a vision of evangelism that is theocentric in character.[26]

The Practices of Christian Witness

As a way of reflecting on some of the new directions taken in the theology of evangelism since the publication of *The Logic of Evangelism*, we will briefly examine two significant contributions by Methodist scholars. First, the work by Scott Jones in *The Evangelistic Love of God and Neighbor* is probably the most significant attempt at explicitly critiquing and extending Abraham's approach while retaining a distinctively Wesleyan trajectory.[27] Second, Bryan Stone's work on *Evangelism after Christendom* pays tribute to Abraham but then goes in another direction in order to develop an approach to Christian witness that is shaped by postliberal theology and Anabaptist ecclesiology.[28]

24. For an interesting approach to the priority of divine agency in evangelism, see Wells, *God the Evangelist*.

25. Abraham, *Logic of Evangelism*, 103–4.

26. Abraham, *Logic of Evangelism*, 98.

27. Jones, *Evangelistic Love of God and Neighbor*, 17–18. Jones was successor to William Abraham as McCreless Professor of Evangelism at Perkins School of Theology.

28. Stone, *Evangelism after Christendom*, 18.

What they all have in common is a reading of evangelism within the theocentric and missional narrative of Christian life under the reign of God. Both enlarge on Abraham's critique of evangelism as proclamation, which aims at making converts, and the machinery of church growth, which truncates the meaning of true discipleship. Where they differ, however, is in their interpretations of how initiation into the kingdom relates to participation in the church and how this participation shapes our witness in the world.

Evangelism as Initiation into the Life of Discipleship

For Jones, the idea of evangelism as initiation into the kingdom of God is too vague to be practically helpful. On the one hand, he argues that *The Logic of Evangelism* tends to identify evangelism with the whole process of making mature and responsible disciples—and so loses the real meaning of initiation as the start of the journey. On the other hand, Jones also says that if the whole ministry of the church is evangelistic in nature, then evangelism as a distinct practice can evaporate and take the whole disciple making enterprise along with it. Jones modifies Abraham's definition to overcome these ambiguities while retaining its central terms: "Evangelism is that set of loving, intentional activities governed by the goal of initiating persons into Christian discipleship in response to the reign of God."[29]

Jones re-appropriates the polymorphous activity outlined by Abraham as ingredients in the process of disciple making and gives evangelism the concrete aim of inviting people to get involved. It is for this reason that he adds the ingredient of faith sharing, since living under the reign of God includes the personal responsibility of communicating the Gospel to others. The love of God and neighbor motivates this witness, and the church offers it as witness through works of mercy, in both word and deed, and invites those who encounter God's reign to make the decision to start the journey of discipleship. And while the experience of conversion is not the immediate goal of faith-sharing or witnessing, it is anticipated within the journey itself through interaction with the disciple-making community. This approach to belonging-before-believing has the advantage of preserving evangelism from reduction to a para-church activity. Experience suggests that unless the church intentionally pursues this radical change of heart, it will neglect this link. Abraham's original proposal has the benefit of

29. Jones, *Evangelistic Love*, 18.

retaining a subtle connection between evangelism and conversion by making it an intentional aspect of initiation into the kingdom. This connection is important.

Jones also identifies an ambiguity in Abraham's language of initiation when it comes to the relationship between the church and the kingdom of God. By making the church an agent of the kingdom, he argues that Abraham essentially conflates initiation into the kingdom with initiation into the church. Instead, he claims, the kingdom is operative throughout the world, and "persons may well be initiated into the reign of God outside the ministry of the church."[30] It is far from clear if Abraham actually makes this mistake or if Jones has something else in mind by making this distinction. Perhaps Jones is implying that the work of evangelism belongs to the church when it is both gathered and scattered throughout the world in the witness of discipleship. If so, this would be an important observation, given the research that points to the significance of personal relationships with non-Christians as a crucial means by which they come to faith.[31]

At various other points, however, Jones asserts that "real Christians are always connected with the church" and that "persons carrying the ministry of evangelism must have a close relationship to the church." Moreover, he says, "ideally it is the church itself that is doing the evangelizing, and part of the initiation process is the invitation to experience life in a local Christian community."[32] In the end, this proposal is at least as ambiguous as that of Abraham, but for different reasons. The work of Bryan Stone offers a radical solution to this ecclesiological issue.

Evangelism as the Embodied Witness of Christian Community

Stone begins his study by arguing that many conceptions of evangelism run the risk of instrumentalization, as we tend to define evangelism in terms of achieving goals such as personal decision, church attendance, and the

30. Jones, *Evangelistic Love*, 73.

31. For research done in the United Kingdom, see Finney, *Finding Faith Today*. The picture in America points to the greater influence of ordained ministry and especially the hospitality of the congregation (See Boston University, "Finding Faith Today"). This might point to the more deeply secular and post-Christian culture of the UK, and the challenges of evangelizing persons whose contact with the church is removed by multiple generations.

32. Jones, *Evangelistic Love*, 81–82, 139.

making of converts or disciples.[33] The danger is that we can subvert our own theocentric aspirations by anthropocentric expectations and become captivated by the mechanistic logic of relevancy, efficiency, and productivity. We can instrumentalize the practice of evangelism when we shape it by striving for measurable outcomes and other metrics of success. From this perspective, even the so-called "logic of initiation" can become captive to instrumentalist thinking. (It is unfortunate that Jones goes out of his way to assert that evangelism is "a process that aims at a product," which can only be the decision to embark on the journey of discipleship. Jones's language here is also part of the problem.)[34]

Therefore, with these issues in mind, it is important to note that Stone changes the whole focus of evangelism from what we do for others, to *who we are in ourselves*. Our witness is not about sharing the Gospel through various methods of verbal communication but rather about embodying the truth of the Gospel in the form of holy living.[35] The "ordinary non-conformity" of authentic discipleship is "the central and defining logic of evangelism," and "the evangelistic invitation is, in the first place, a matter of living beautifully and truthfully before a watching world."[36] Moreover, we cannot reduce witness to the kingdom to personal strategies of faith sharing because it is in the social reality of the church that God makes God's reign visible and tangible. Therefore, if Jones is concerned that Abraham draws too close a connection between the kingdom and the church, Stone leaves us wondering whether he makes it close enough.

For Stone, evangelism is fundamentally an ecclesiological issue. It is nothing other than the church's faithful witness to the reign of God by embodying the virtues of the kingdom in the character of our community and the quality of our relationships. He says, "The practice of evangelism is a complex and multilayered process, a context of multiple activities that invite, herald, welcome, and provoke and that has as its end the peaceable reign of God and the social holiness by which people are oriented toward that reign."[37] Apparently, we are not to aim the practice of evangelism at changing the lives of others but at having *our own hearts and lives transformed* by the kingdom-shaped and Spirit-filled disciplines of the church.

33. Stone, *After Christendom*, 16.

34. Jones, *Evangelistic Love*, 104.

35. Stone, *After Christendom*, 230–55.

36. Stone, *After Christendom*, 314–15.

37. Stone, *After Christendom*, 316.

Through encountering the beauty of holiness, we will taste the goodness of God and voluntarily submit our lives to the reign of God by joining the Christian community. We will then extend this witness to the world through the holy lives of saints and martyrs, through whom others will come and see the truth of the kingdom in the extraordinary way we love God and one another.[38]

From this perspective, conversion is neither a momentary experience produced by evangelistic methods nor the by-product of disciple-making activities. It is the long process of being conformed by the Spirit to a new way of life in Christ through participation in a community of virtuous practice.[39] There is no room for solitary Christianity, individualistic piety, or private spirituality in this vision of evangelism. It is unfortunate, however, that Stone tends to throw out the evangelical language of personal relationship with God with the bathwater of individualistic and consumerist spirituality. Emphasizing the social reality of the kingdom does not entail losing the irreducibly personal nature of our decision to follow Jesus as Spirit-filled children of the living God. Indeed, without the indwelling of the Spirit of Christ as the source and goal of our witness, the pursuit of social holiness can slide into the mere form of religion, and there is no power for evangelistic mission.

The Gift of the Evangelist

The works of Abraham, Jones, and Stone aim to provide a vision for the theology and practice of evangelism. And yet, as we have noted, there is a danger in contributing more to the field of academic theology than the church's practice of evangelistic mission. I would like to suggest, however, that these works could also help us to diagnose the reasons behind the "evangelism gap" in the first place and to consider how we might close it.

Minding the Gap

First, Scott Jones helps us identify the gap between knowing the Gospel and sharing our faith. Here, it is significant to know *what* the Gospel is, and we might even know *how* we can share it with others in word and deed. The

---

38. Stone, *After Christendom*, 279–85.

39. Stone, *After Christendom*, 258–63.

problem is that we do not do what we know we should do! We must consider the proposal that Jones makes for personal witness as faith-sharing as a vital starting point for the process of making disciples and for the way we need to "empower laity to witness verbally."[40] Jones carefully explains the forms this witness can take, but he does not explain how they are to be embodied when opportunities arise.

Second, Bryan Stone helps us identify the gap between knowing the Gospel and holy living. We might know *what* kind of people the Gospel calls us to be, and we might even know *how* God can make our lives and churches beautiful from the inside out. The problem is that we do not make the pursuit of holiness a priority! The argument Stone makes for the social holiness of the church and the personal holiness of saintly disciples is vital to the credibility of the Gospel. He carefully explains what this holy witness looks like, but he does not explain how the church is to pursue it or how the church is to avoid conformity with the world. Moreover, Stone seems to separate holy living and faith sharing. Here, we must insist that we cannot be authentic witnesses apart from sharing the Gospel; we make the Gospel plausible by the character witness we offer to the world. Therefore, there is an inseparable connection between holy living and faith sharing; when we gather as a Christian community and when we scatter into the world as disciples, we make a witness to the Gospel. Indeed, holy living is the Gospel made audible, visible, and tangible in the lives of Christians and churches, but faith-sharing is the way we point others to the true source of faith in God.

Closing the Gap

I want to argue that the church can close this multi-layered evangelism gap by taking up Abraham's convictions about the need to re-evangelize the church. I do not mean that we need a fresh wave of revival meetings to make real Christians out of nominal church members—although that may be necessary! Rather, I mean that we need to recognize and embrace those with the gift of evangelism whom Christ "equips for such works of service" (Eph 4:11–12). Although we now have substantial works on the theology and practice of evangelism, there is little scholarship on the gift and role of the evangelist.[41]

---

40. Jones, *Evangelistic Love of God*, 197.

41. For a helpful start, see Gehring, *Oxbridge Evangelist.* The book is based on a PhD

We have seen that Abraham identifies "the evangelist" as one of four agents in evangelism, but the nature of that role remains somewhat underdeveloped. On the one hand, he provides a robust critique of reducing evangelism to proclamation, but he still tends to reduce the role of evangelist to this task.[42] On the other hand, he can tend to relativize the role of "evangelist" to include every other gift of ministry that might intentionally serve the goal of initiation into the kingdom of God.[43] For sure, the work of an evangelist is to proclaim the gospel, even with signs and wonders. Equipping the church for the work of evangelism, however, means helping the church "become mature, attaining to the whole measure of the fullness of Christ" (Eph 4:13). This "fullness" means the pursuit of holiness, as those who live worthy of the calling they have received in Christ. It means sharing the gospel as those who join the mission of Christ to announce the present and future reign of God before an unbelieving world.

How does the evangelist accomplish this task, and what is the nature of the spiritual gift for building up the church? First, those with the gift of evangelist will close the gap between knowing the Gospel and sharing faith through their own personal example and by apprenticing others in the art of faithful witness. Second, they will close the gap between knowing the Gospel and holy living by their own pursuit of holiness and holding others accountable by "speaking the truth in love" (Eph 4:25). Third, I suggest that we reconnect holy living and faith-sharing through the practice of disciplined Christian fellowship. For example, those with the gift of evangelism are likely to model what it means to pursue a life of holy love through the art of spiritual conversation. This unity of living and speaking the gospel will be catalyzed in small groups, then spread through the whole church and out into to the world. Finally, we cannot think of evangelism as initiating people into the kingdom or the life of discipleship without having a Gospel-shaped community to receive them. We will need to characterize those with the gift of evangelism by a zealous love for God and neighbor compelled by a love to share the Gospel with the least and the lost. This zeal is the flame of holy love that burns in the heart and kindles the same passion in others for the kingdom. It is only with this passion that the whole ministry of the church will become evangelistic by nature and find its common purpose in the evangelistic mission of God.

thesis co-supervised by William Abraham and myself.

42. Abraham, *Logic of Evangelism*, 172, 203–7, 229–32.

43. Abraham, *Logic of Evangelism*, 106–7.

I find myself deeply thankful for *The Logic of Evangelism* and the field it has helped to define. In my view, it is still the single best treatment of evangelism. There may be other works in evangelist theory and practice, such as those I have cited and explored; they have provided some helpful nuances and furthered key aspects of my argument. But we will still need to define evangelism "after Abraham" as initiation into the kingdom of God, though perhaps viewed as a holistic journey of discipleship and with a greater emphasis on the embodied witness of the disciple-making community. My modest proposal for greater attention to the role of evangelist does not add anything to this theory but simply asks how we may more fully realize it in practice.

Chapter Two

The Gospel:
Abraham's Kingdom Evangelism

Scott J. Jones

William J. Abraham's greatest accomplishment in *The Logic of Evangelism* was directing attention to the definition of the term "evangelism." For a word that has played such an important role in twentieth-century American Christianity, its level of imprecision in usage is astonishing. Abraham's opening chapter discusses the "rift between evangelism and theology." He noted that most books on evangelism do not seriously address theological issues and that "the best intellectual efforts of the Christian community are channeled into fields that either elbow out or inhibit serious engagement with the topic of evangelism." He concludes:

> The reason for our difficulties in this area goes much deeper, however. Even if we were sure that the great theologians had something interesting to say about evangelism, something we should surely assume as true until proven otherwise, we face a perplexing dilemma. We do not know what precisely to define as evangelism and therefore we are at a loss as to know what to designate as a contribution to a discussion about it.[1]

This situation has led and, unfortunately, continues to lead to deep confusion in conversations about evangelism.

Abraham's focus on defining the term made a major contribution in theological literature because it raised the question of how this area of

---

1. Abraham, *Logic of Evangelism*, 7.

16

Christian ministry should be defined. While others did not necessarily adopt his specific proposal, his attention to the definitional issues changed the conversation from that point forward.

Materially, his second chapter, entitled "The Gospel," put forward his major contribution to the study of evangelism, a focus on the kingdom of God. He begins with a bold claim:

> Any considered attempt to develop a coherent concept of evange- lism that will be serviceable in the present must begin with escha- tology. Whatever evangelism may be, it is at least intimately related to the gospel of the reign of God that was inaugurated in the life, death, and resurrection of Jesus of Nazareth. Any vision of evan- gelism that ignores the kingdom of God, or relegates it to a posi- tion of secondary importance, or fails to wrestle thoroughly with its content is destined at the outset to fail. This is so because the kingdom of God is absolutely central to the ministry of Jesus and to the mission of the disciples that launched the Christian move- ment into history. What is not at stake here is the prevalence of the idea of the kingdom of God in the biblical writings, although that could be argued persuasively. What is at stake is the fundamental theological horizon within which Jesus and his followers conceive and carry out the first, and paradigmatic, evangelistic action of the church. This cannot be the last word but rather must be the first word on evangelism.[2]

Abraham is boldly asserting the primacy of eschatology for evangelism. His rationale is based on a two-fold argument. First, it is the ministry of Jesus and the disciples that must determine our understanding of evangelism. Without explicitly claiming a textual priority for his analysis, he focuses mostly on the synoptic gospels as his biblical source. Second, Abraham ar- gues that Jesus' ministry was best understood as shaped by the announce- ment that God's kingdom was at hand.

He recognizes that the concept of the kingdom of God is contested and he outlines three broad positions. The first option interprets Jesus' ministry as pointing toward a future kingdom which was expected to break into history soon. Abraham references the work of Johannes Weiss and Albert Schweitzer and notes that the delay of the second coming posed problems for the earliest generations of Christians.

The second proposal suggests that the kingdom had already come in Jesus' ministry. C. H. Dodd's advocacy of a realized eschatology built on

2. Abraham, *Logic of Evangelism*, 17.

references to the kingdom being already present and said that the eternally present kingdom was tied to Jesus' ministry.

The third proposal is a combination of the two. It argues for the present reality of the kingdom as well as its future fulfillment. Abraham favors "some version" of this option. Essential to this view is his reliance on an understanding of how God has acted, is acting and will act in human history:

> God's reign has begun; he has come in Jesus to bring judgment and liberation; he comes repeatedly in history in salvation and discipline; his rule is within reach of both individuals and nations; we can now enter into its penultimate inauguration as we strive toward its full and final consummation. Yet there is more to come; what we experience now is a foretaste and foreshadowing of those ultimate acts of God that will bring history to its teleological denouement at the great and manifest day of the Lord, which is beyond literal description.[3]

Abraham sees that the primary agent, although not the only agent, in the evangelistic process is God.[4] He does not shy away from descriptions of how God interacts with creation and how God's activity is connected with the ministries of other agents. The church, the evangelist, and the person being evangelized—all are involved in the process. Yet, he is clear: "Evangelism should be housed very firmly within the dynamic rule of God on earth. This will provide fresh conceptuality for grasping its fundamental nature and new inspiration for its practice."[5] On his description, the kingdom of God is the overall category for describing what God is doing in the world. He can balance the "already come" approach to the kingdom with a perspective that it will be completely fulfilled at some future time. He says:

> Eschatology is a vision of the coming of the kingdom of God that was initiated in Jesus of Nazareth, was experienced and cherished by the community that arose after his death and resurrection, and is now within the grasp of those who will repent and receive the gift of the Holy Spirit; yet it remains to come in all its glory and fullness. . . . Moreover, evangelism is an activity of the followers of Jesus that should be rooted and grounded in this dynamic, mysterious, numinous reality of the rule of God in history.[6]

3. Abraham, *Logic of Evangelism*, 34–35.

4. Abraham, *Logic of Evangelism*, 103.

5. Abraham, *Logic of Evangelism*, 18.

6. Abraham, *Logic of Evangelism*, 38–39.

Abraham has had a long-standing interest in the theology of divine action. He has made a number of contributions to studies of that topic, including a two-volume work, *Divine Agency* and *Divine Action*. In *The Logic of Evangelism*, he addresses several concerns that "hover in the neighborhood." First, he says that the coming of the kingdom is often hidden and open to divergent interpretations: "God works mysteriously as well as openly in the establishment of his rule so that to demand prepackaged signs and wonders is to miss the possibility of his action here and now in the mundane events of history."[7]

Abraham seeks to carve out a balanced approach to the kingdom that avoids mistakes made by other theologians:

> Where both liberal and existentialist theologies have erred is not so much in what they have affirmed but in what they have denied. Working out of incomplete and inadequate accounts of eschatology, they have tended to confine God's coming to their favorite hunting grounds for divine action. They have lost sight of the sophisticated link between present and future that is at the heart of eschatology and thus they tended to collapse the whole of eschatology into the present. By restoring the inner logic of God's action as it embraces past, present, and future, we can build upon their insights without embracing their costly errors.[8]

He is quite aware that this chapter does not present a complete account of eschatology. Rather, the goal of this discussion is to create sufficient conceptual space so that he can define evangelism as initiation into the kingdom.

Abraham's move here addresses some of the more popular misconceptions about eschatology, such as the apocalyptic expectations that some have about an imminent end of the world. Such expectations arise partly from the confusion about literal and metaphorical language but also from the great joy, delight, and hope found when one experiences the coming of God's reign in one's own life.[9]

The experience of the kingdom was the sufficient motivation for the early church to evangelize. The spread of Christianity was not the result of a program or the work of professional preachers. Rather:

> The church grew because the sovereign hand of God was in the midst of the community that found itself surrounded by people

7. Abraham, *Logic of Evangelism*, 33.

8. Abraham, *Logic of Evangelism*, 34.

9. Abraham, *Logic of Evangelism*, 35.

who were puzzled and intrigued by what they saw happening. The overwhelming impression created by the traditions witnessing to the early evangelistic activity of the disciples is that the Holy Spirit was present in the community, bringing in the reign of God and inspiring the disciples to speak boldly of the mighty acts of salvation that God had wrought through the life, death, and resurrection of Jesus.[10]

Strengths

Given that a crucial task is to define evangelism, Abraham's proposal that it be "rooted and grounded in this dynamic, mysterious, numinous reality of the rule of God in history" has three important strengths.[11]

First, Abraham's choice of the kingdom of God as a crucial concept around which to build his definition has a strong biblical basis. One of the most important aspects of any theological argument is its starting point. There is no doubt that the kingdom was crucial to the ministry of Jesus, the apostles, and the early church. To begin at the point where Jesus began his ministry provides a very strong foundation for the rest of his proposal. Evangelism's etymological root is the Greek word "euangelion." At the very beginning of Mark's Gospel, the word appears. While it is used in Mark 1:1 to introduce the book, the earliest description of Jesus' preaching makes reference to the "euangelion" and the kingdom of God. It says:

> Now after John was arrested, Jesus came to Galilee, proclaiming the good news of God, and saying, "The time is fulfilled, and the kingdom of God has come near; repent, and believe in the good news." (Mark 1:14–15, NRSV)

This strong biblical basis gives significant credibility to the idea that evangelism should be tied directly to Jesus' preaching about the inbreaking kingdom of God. When the church asks, "How should we think about evangelism?" an appeal to the ministry of Jesus is one of the best possible arguments. Surely, following Jesus should mean bearing witness to the same message he proclaimed.

Second, placing the kingdom of God at the center of thinking about evangelism has an added benefit: it grounds the work of initiation broadly

---

10. Abraham, *Logic of Evangelism*, 38.

11. Abraham, *Logic of Evangelism*, 39.

in the totality of God's activity in the world. For most of the twentieth century, American churches have been polarized by a division between those who favor a social gospel of pursuing justice and an individual gospel of conversion to belief in Christ. As Abraham makes clear, the reign of God involves individual transformation as well as the pursuit of social justice. Many writers about the church's pursuit of social justice have relied on the reign of God as a crucial concept. Abraham's kingdom initiation proposal is an important way to link the theology of evangelism with other theological disciplines. It also can be used to build connections between various theological camps.

Third, it names God as the primary agent and accounts for the power of personal and social transformation. Too often, Christians focus on human agency as the crucial factor in evangelism. Earlier writers (one might think of Charles Finney) tried to reduce the process of converting sinners to a few repeatable steps. Abraham's focus on divine action correctly reminds those thinking about evangelism that salvation is, first and foremost, by God's amazing grace.

This focus on God's agency has the added benefit of capturing the motivation and spiritual context for evangelism. Throughout Christian history, it has been a fresh vision of God's saving activity that has led to powerful evangelistic progress. Abraham's reminder that this activity is both present and future while simultaneously perceived and hidden is crucial.

Fourth, his focus on the kingdom of God lays a very helpful foundation for his six components of the Christian life described in chapters six and seven. After describing initiation, Abraham notes that the kingdom involves conversion, baptism, morality, the creed, spiritual gifts, and disciplines. Such a varied list requires some unifying concept and the kingdom provides that for his proposal.

Weaknesses

Three crucial weaknesses hinder the overall adequacy of Abraham's proposal.

First, it is rooted in too narrow a biblical basis. There is no doubt that the in-breaking reign of God was central to Jesus' ministry. Focusing on a theory of evangelism gains much strength from this concept and its centrality to the Synoptic Gospels. But Abraham does not make a case that this concept is the main, unifying theme of the whole Bible. What should an account of the general tenor of scripture look like?

David Kelsey in his *Uses of Scripture in Recent Theology* makes an important point about the wholeness of Scripture for theologians. He reviews the work of several quite different theologians and concludes:

> [The cases studies] showed that when a theologian tries to authorize a theological proposal by appeal to scripture he is obliged to decide what it is *in* scripture that is authoritative. On closer examination, moreover, it turned out that what he appeals to are certain *patterns* characteristically exhibited by the aspect of scripture he takes to be authoritative. When a text is construed in terms of such a pattern, it is construed as though that pattern constitutes a whole whose unity is analogous to that of some other familiar kind of literature.

In every case, when a theologian appeals to scripture to help authorize a theological proposal, he appeals not just to some aspect of scripture but to a *pattern* characteristically exhibited by that aspect of scripture, and in virtue of that pattern, he construes the scripture to which he appeals as some kind of *whole*. Part of what it means to call a set of texts "authoritative scripture" is to ascribe to it some kind of wholeness or unity when it is used as authority.[12]

Precisely because evangelism is about the gospel, it is important that a theology of evangelism appeal to the whole scripture. It should reference the pattern of meaning embedded in both testaments. Abraham brings a categorical, general claim in his first and third sentences of the chapter:

> Any considered attempt to develop a coherent concept of evangelism that will be serviceable in the present must begin with eschatology. . . . Any vision of evangelism that ignores the kingdom of God, or relegates it to a position of secondary importance, or fails to wrestle thoroughly with its content is destined at the outset to fail.[13]

This claim is far from self-evident, and a careful reading of chapter two leaves the reader wondering if he has in fact established the necessary priority for eschatology as the beginning place. Abraham's second sentence is more nuanced: "Whatever evangelism may be, it is at least intimately related to the gospel of the reign of God that was inaugurated in the life,

12. Kelsey, *Uses of Scripture*, 101–2.

13. Abraham, *Logic of Evangelism*, 17.

death, and resurrection of Jesus of Nazareth."[14] It is a very different claim to say that any coherent view of evangelism must begin with eschatology than to say that any such view of evangelism must include the kingdom of God in a significant place.

Kelsey's analysis shows that there are many ways of construing the wholeness of scripture and deciding which parts of scripture we ought to see as the hermeneutical key for discerning that pattern. His perspective shows that a more persuasive argument for any theory of evangelism must wrestle with the totality of scripture.

For example, John Wesley viewed the general tenor of Scripture as being constituted by "that grand scheme of doctrine which is delivered therein touch original sin, justification by faith and present, inward salvation."[15] In many of his sermons, Wesley talked about the way of salvation as being composed of stages such as the three outlined here, sometimes adding repentance and sanctification to the list.[16] In "The Way to the Kingdom," he gives an interpretation of the kingdom of God that builds in a broader understanding of discipleship than is evident in Abraham's work, in part because he cites Pauline letters as well as the Synoptic Gospels. Citing Wesley's understanding of the whole scripture is not in and of itself authoritative, but it illustrates that attentiveness to the wholeness of scripture can lead to different conclusions. In particular, I have argued that the Great Commission's focus on discipleship provides a better way of attending to the whole Bible's message. My proposal was to define the heart of evangelism as initiation into Christian discipleship in response to the reign of God.[17] All of this suggests that Abraham has not sufficiently made his argument for the centrality of eschatology.

Second, Abraham argues in a later chapter that initiation is a crucial part of his conception of evangelism. This comes much closer to an analytic judgment that cannot be contradicted. Whatever evangelism is, it surely involves entry into something and a change in one's life. However, entry of an individual into the kingdom of God is never well defined. Abraham is clear that God's action in the world constitutes an inbreaking of God's rule and that it has consequences for both individuals and the world as a whole, but it is not clear that if the kingdom is taking over how that constitutes entry

14. Abraham, *Logic of Evangelism*, 17.

15. Wesley, *Explanatory Notes*, Romans 12:6.

16. See Jones, *John Wesley's Conception and Use of Scripture*, 22.

17. Jones, *Evangelistic Love*, 114.

for the individuals affected. If the kingdom comes into a situation, one's context might be altered, one might experience God in powerful ways, or one might be affected in a variety of ways. Initiation into discipleship or into a new community in response to such an experience is easily understood. The inbreaking of the kingdom as an event which requires initiation seems to be missing some vital components of the definition.

Summary

Abraham's focus on the definition of evangelism and his linkage to the kingdom of God constitutes an important contribution to the study of evangelism. It changed the discussion among academics and pointed many others toward a deeper and more comprehensive understanding. Whatever improvements others have made since its publication, we stand indebted to this groundbreaking work.

Chapter Three

Proclamation

KIMBERLY D. REISMAN

AT THE INTERSECTION OF scholarship and the life of the church, few people have been as influential as William Abraham. Writing at a time when evangelism was a fringe discussion in scholarly circles rather than a legitimate topic of conversation, Abraham lifted the study of evangelism to the level of serious theological inquiry. Therefore, it is not out of bounds to suggest that the publication of *The Logic of Evangelism* elevated the field of evangelism to such a degree that a new generation of scholars was birthed and an important new body of scholarship created.

In offering a larger conceptualization of evangelism, Abraham provided a springboard for discussion of evangelism, most of which engaged with his framework of evangelism as initiation.[1] His desire to bring clarity and understanding resonated with both scholars and practitioners alike; and, though different in detail, much of the scholarship that followed the publication of *The Logic of Evangelism* accepted Abraham's understanding that evangelism involved more than proclamation alone.

Recently, however, there has been renewed interest in developing theologies of evangelism that more thoroughly engage the role of proclamation. Rather than see the challenge as requiring an expansion of what constitutes evangelism as a whole, these scholars believe that a more systematic understanding of evangelism as proclamation is in order.[2] It is a

1. See Chilcote and Warner, *Study of Evangelism*; Heath, *Mystic Way of Evangelism*; Heath and Kisker, *Longing for Spring*; Jones, *Evangelistic Love*; and Warner, *Saving Women*.

2. See Jackson, *Wesleyan Theology of Evangelism*.

testament to the lasting impact of Abraham's work and to the heightened level of scholarship now expected in the study of evangelism that the desire to reclaim a privileged role for proclamation exists. *The Logic of Evangelism* has elevated new theological exploration as well as become a crucial text to engage new approaches in the practice of evangelism.

To be sure, Abraham's work has impacted the field of evangelism. I know I have been encouraged by the ongoing interaction among scholars and practioners. It has been beneficial to see how the conversation, particularly as it relates to proclamation, has been taking place and how evangelism is on the radar, especially in the academy. Abraham's groundbreaking work has opened up new territory.

Evangelism as Initiation

Before exploring this new territory, however, it is important to review Abraham's understanding of proclamation with respect to evangelism. Because Abraham argues for a broadened conception of the practice of evangelism, his first step is to communicate how evangelism is exclusively proclamation. For Abraham, "Limiting evangelism to the mere proclamation of the gospel is artificial."[3] His critique involves several assertions, one of which limits evangelism to proclamation.[4] And though proclamation is singled out, due to its crucial nature, the emphasis in itself is not sufficient to determine that was all the early evangelists did.[5] John Wesley is also an example; though he was itinerant in his preaching, he was also fully committed to "not only proclaiming the gospel but seeing that those who responded were converted, established in the faith, incorporated into class meetings, and related to the local parish."[6]

A second argument against defining evangelism solely as proclamation is that, in the modern Western world, doing so essentially cuts evangelism loose from Christian communities. For the early church, evangelism and community were intimately connected. Not so in our postmodern setting, where a dramatic emphasis on individual autonomy, coupled with antipathy toward community and tradition, makes the challenge to link evangelism with life in the body of Christ difficult to overcome. At the time

3. Abraham, *Logic of Evangelism*, 55.
4. Abraham, *Logic of Evangelism*, 50–51.
5. Abraham, *Logic of Evangelism*, 54.
6. Abraham, *Logic of Evangelism*, 54.

Abraham wrote *The Logic of Evangelism*, the prevailing view in the church is that evangelism is a still ministry distinct from the regular life of the community of faith; it is an arena for experts, occurring at special times and places. Abraham's work to construe evangelism as proclamation alone simply "clings to the wrong kind of verbal continuity with the past."[7]

We can see Abraham's key point for broadening understanding of evangelism beyond proclamation alone in his opposition to the anthropocentric focus of much evangelistic preaching over the last two hundred years. The focus on the response of the individual has been, and often continues to be, paramount; rather than being filtered through the lens of the kingdom of God announced by Jesus of Nazareth, the content of proclamation has become exclusively soteriological, narrowing salvation of the individual sinner.[8]

Closely connected to this concern is Abraham's critique about the way the mass media continues to shape modern communication and proclamation. The danger here, he states, is the absence of the "numinous reality of the Holy Spirit that is present in the lives of those who announce the coming of the kingdom."[9] For Abraham, evangelism is more than communication to isolated individuals because it is "a matter of the power of the living God, unveiling himself to the minds and hearts of the listener as the gospel is taught and made known."[10] This hyper-anthropocentrism, together with the absence of the "vital, mysterious dimension" of the Holy Spirit, is one of the worst features of modern evangelism. It is why Abraham is not convinced the remedy for this failure focuses solely on verbal proclamation.[11] Abraham writes as follows:

> Above all, what is important is to combat the isolation of evangelism from the full ministry of the church and to rescue it from the shallow anthropocentrism and individualism into which it has tumbled in the last two centuries. *This does not mean that we abandon the crucial significance of proclamation in evangelism*, but it does mean that we enrich our conception of evangelism to include the vital first phases of initiation into the kingdom of God.[12]

7. Abraham, *Logic of Evangelism*, 57.

8. Abraham, *Logic of Evangelism*, 58–59.

9. Abraham, *Logic of Evangelism*, 60.

10. Abraham, *Logic of Evangelism*, 60.

11. Abraham, *Logic of Evangelism*, 61.

12. Abraham, *Logic of Evangelism*, 69. Emphasis added.

Abraham as Interlocutor

The increase in academic scholarship around the study of evangelism in the years since the release of *The Logic of Evangelism* continues to make Abraham's work an outstanding partner and interlocutor, especially in the Wesleyan tradition. In my own doctoral studies, for instance, I shared Abraham's frustration with the anthropomorphic focus in evangelism. His observation that "much of modern mass evangelism has reached such a nadir of public scandal and disorder" prompted serious theological reflection.[13] I recall during my research how my husband and I encountered an acquaintance at an art gallery. We knew each other from community work. As we introduced our spouses, my acquaintance mentioned how I was working on my PhD, but he could not remember the area of study. When I responded the "theology of evangelism," our friends recoiled in horror in perfect tandem. The husband realized the visible reaction of the response and quickly tried to recover. "Evangelism?" he said, "I never would have thought. You've always struck me as so open-minded and compassionate." It is clear that even long after the publication of *The Logic of Evangelism*, the persistence of such negative associations with evangelism makes Abraham's reference to the problems of moral corruption of public or television evangelists all the more gripping.

It is why Abraham's idea that evangelistic effort is not complete until people are firmly rooted in the kingdom of God has been such a significant touchstone in my doctoral work as I developed a Trinitarian theological grounding for evangelism.[14] As an evangelist in the larger Wesleyan world, I am consistently in the role of "verbal proclaimer" of the gospel. In this new role, I am always interested in how I may engage and build upon Abraham's understanding of evangelism, not only in relation to an overarching theology of evangelism but also regarding how the church can work to establish persons in the faith.

New Theological Voices

On the academic front, Jack Jackson is a Wesleyan scholar who engages Abraham in the fashion we have been outlining. In contrast to Abraham's

---

13. Abraham, *Logic of Evangelism*, 10.

14. Reisman, "Evangelism as Embrace of the Other."

desire to broaden the concept of evangelism, Jackson wants to narrow the definition of evangelism to verbal proclamation.[15]

To be sure, there are significant differences between Jackson and Abraham. Where Abraham sees proclamation as one, albeit important, part of evangelism and argues for defining evangelism as "that set of intentional activities which is governed by the goal of initiating people into the kingdom of God for the first time,"[16] Jackson defines evangelism as entirely focused on verbal proclamation.[17] Though I neither wish to downplay the serious disagreement between these two scholars nor ignore the way in which Jackson argues against Abraham's definition, it is not within the scope of this project to undertake a thorough comparison of their positions. However, a cursory reading of both scholars does reveal several key points of overlap: 1) both share similar theological commitments, 2) both have similar methodological approaches, and 3) both have a deep love of the church's ministry.

These similarities provide intriguing insights. For example, both Jackson and Abraham are firmly committed to seeing people established in the kingdom of God, the true end of all evangelistic effort. For Abraham, this establishment is expressed in terms of initiation; for Jackson, it is expressed in his understanding of the progressive responses to the preaching of the word through various stages of discipleship (e.g., awakening, conversion, and Christian perfection). In addition, both scholars recognize the crucial role of the Holy Spirit, without whose power and activity evangelism is impotent and transformation impossible. And finally, both Jackson and Abraham claim the importance of the nature of the community of faith as the crucible in which evangelism must take place.[18]

But there is more. We can also note the impact of Abraham's *The Logic of Evangelism* on Jackson's scholarship, especially with respect to the emphasis on creating a systematic and logical scheme for understanding evangelism: e.g., where Abraham focuses on a conceptualization of evangelism as initiation, Jackson offers a systematic and "nuanced understanding of proclamation and the appropriate response(s)" to it.[19] There is no doubt Abraham would agree with such a systematic development of proclama-

---

15. Jackson, *Proclamation*, 104.

16. Abraham, *Logic of Evangelism*, 95.

17. Jackson, *Proclamation*, 104.

18 Abraham, *Logic of Evangelism*, 96–100, and Jackson, *Proclamation*, 100–2.

19. Jackson, *Proclamation*, 105.

tion and how such a development can help to deepen our understanding of evangelism, whether it is defined more broadly as initiation or more narrowly as proclamation.[20]

Such comparison is important, as both Jackson and Abraham avoid the modern temptation of an "individualistic understanding of evangelism that is primarily, if not only, concerned with conversion, and which fails to adequately emphasize initiation, social ministry, discipleship, and mission in new Christians."[21] Abraham's confluence with Jackson becomes clear here as Abraham demands that we take the complex and nuanced nature of the Christian faith seriously, especially with its communal dimensions. By arguing for evangelism as initiation, Abraham seeks a deeper understanding of what it means to be initiated into the kingdom of God. Such initiation, he asserts, will have "its own internal grammar, its own internal structure, constraints, and logic," a very communal aspect.[22] He elaborates on this logic by attending to the ways the church practices conversion, baptism, morality, the creed, spiritual gifts, and discipline.

In similar systematic fashion, Jackson challenges us to move beyond both stereotypical and metaphorical interpretations of proclamation in evangelism by offering a scheme of criteria, modes, and responses; that is, Jackson argues for a logical set of criteria for understanding evangelism as proclamation, criteria which include content, response, the presence of the Holy Spirit, a speaker, roots in a community of faith, audience, and social setting. He then elaborates what he calls "four modes of evangelism" as well: e.g., preaching, witnessing, Christian education (teaching) and worship.[23] Jackson argues that when persons experience the church's ministry of evangelism in these various modes, there are three responses, depending on the stage of discipleship: for instance, awakening, conversion, and Christian perfection. Together, Jackson's scheme provides an equally nuanced and multifaceted conception of evangelism, despite what appears to be a limited definition of it as proclamation.

20. Jackson, *Proclamation*, 135.

21. Jackson, *Proclamation*, 157–58.

22. Abraham, *Logic of Evangelism*, 96.

23. Jackson, *Proclamation*, 105.

Irony in Evangelism

As we engage Abraham and Jackson's seemingly opposing views in evangelism, we begin to see a subtle irony emerge: as Jackson disagrees with Abraham's understanding of evangelism as initiation and seeks to narrow the definition to proclamation alone—by following Abraham's lead in employing a systematic, multifaceted, and nuanced approach—Jackson's interpretation of evangelism as proclamation also begins to become broader, multifaceted, and nuanced. In other words, where Abraham has an expanded definition of evangelism as initiation, Jackson also has an expanded conception of evangelism as focusing on the modes of preaching, Christian Education (teaching), witnessing, and worship.[24]

At this point, we can see how both Jackson and Abraham are firmly aligned in desiring clarity about what is and is not evangelism. We cannot, for instance, consider all verbal communication as evangelistic—a point on which they both agree. And yet, for Jackson, proclamation is not limited to preaching and neither is evangelism—a point with which Abraham would agree. Rather, the intersection of Jackson's discussion of the ingredients of proclamation and the modes of evangelism provide an additional example of Abraham's influence on Jackson, despite the fact that Jackson moves his argument in a different direction. For both scholars, proclamation is not evangelism unless it is focused on "the good news of Christ's lordship and inauguration of the kingdom through his life, death, and resurrection."[25] The theological horizon of the kingdom inaugurated by Jesus Christ, crucified and risen from the dead, is what constitutes the church's evangelistic mission. It provides the fuel or passion to offset the anthropocentric preaching of the last two hundred years and serves as an offset to the postmodern relativism of the conversational preaching movement of the later part of the twentieth century.[26] To be sure, there is a desire that the church makes known the fullness of the gospel, but there is also a clear concern on the part of both Jackson and Abraham that the church avoid proclaiming a truncated gospel, subsuming the power of salvation to the individual or relativizing the text to the community. In either case, the kingdom is eclipsed.

24. Jackson, *Proclamation*, 127.

25. Jackson, *Proclamation*, 135.

26. The conversation movement in preaching is a movement that seeks to make the gospel relevant through "casual" conversation rather than preaching. We may find such "preaching" in mostly white and upper middle class congregations.

Before moving to the final area of notable convergence between Abraham and Jackson, we need to share a brief word about an aspect of evangelism where there is significant divergence: discipleship. For Abraham, evangelism is initiation into the kingdom of God *for the first time.*[27] It is why he distinguishes clearly between establishing or grounding people in the kingdom of God and then sustaining and nurturing them in discipleship.[28] Abraham wants us to realize how persons, initially grounded in faith, can later fall away and how the ministries offered to bring folks back to faith would not be considered evangelism. Abraham writes:

> Clearly, the Christian life is one of lifelong development and learning; there is always a need for deeper and expanding appropriation of the Christian tradition, for growth in grace, for the development of one's gifts and abilities, and so on. These cannot take place, however, without the kind of fundamental initiation that I am insisting is integral to evangelism. Our present situation is thoroughly unsatisfactory. On the one side, current forms of evangelism tend to offer a reduced version of the gospel and call for very little by way of serious commitment. On the other side, Christian educators tend to shy away from evangelism, trusting that the familial or social environment will supply all that is needed to get Christian nurture on the road to success. The results are predictable: "born again" Christians remain anemic and only marginally, if at all, related to the church catholic; church members remain nominally and barely socialized into the privileges and responsibilities of the kingdom of God.[29]

Abraham's distinction is important as he seeks clarity between two essential concepts: evangelism and discipleship. The problem, according to Jackson, is that Abraham's distinction is not precise enough. Jackson rejects Abraham's descriptor of evangelism "for the first time" and argues that evangelism and discipleship coincide, with evangelism taking place across various stages of discipleship, and with possible responses, including awakening, conversion, and Christian perfection. This divergence is critical in terms of the way both Abraham and Jackson conceive of evangelism.

27. Abraham, *Logic of Evangelism*, 95.
28. Abraham, *Logic of Evangelism*, 108.
29. Abraham, *Logic of Evangelism*, 108.

Final Convergence

And yet, it is this last contrast that provides a segue into the final surprising convergence between Abraham and Jackson, one that is all the more striking given Jackson's clear rejection of Abraham's position. That convergence relates to what Abraham refers to as initiation. Abraham expands evangelism to include a wide range of activities, all governed by the goal of initiation. Jackson, on the other hand, expands the scope of evangelistic effort by incorporating it into the entire discipleship process. Therefore, while Jackson's definition of evangelism remains narrowly focused on verbal proclamation, the *context* of evangelistic activity is broadened to include the wide spectrum of Christian spiritual growth. Jackson sums up this expansion:

> Evangelism as proclamation in the Wesleyan theology of evangelism is an ongoing act of ministry and discipleship. Evangelism is not limited to conversion or initiating people into discipleship, the kingdom, or the church but is rather a constant act of proclaiming the gospel, by people and to people, in partnership with the Holy Spirit. It calls people to respond in faith regardless of their status as disciples, all the time remembering that the goal of discipleship is Christian perfection.[30]

Again, a subtle irony emerges: Abraham, by offering an expanded vision for evangelism as initiation, set the stage for an emphasis on the full integration of persons into the kingdom of God; Jackson, though narrowing evangelism to proclamation alone, stands on that same stage by expanding the *context* of evangelistic effort to include not only those who are just awakening to Christ, but those who have experienced Christian perfection, a depth of discipleship which is hard to imagine as not including being fully initiated into the kingdom of God.

As I reflect on the impact of *The Logic of Evangelism*, particularly in light of work on proclamation by scholars such as Jack Jackson, I cannot help but wonder if Abraham might reconsider if he was too harsh on the role of proclamation in evangelism or, perhaps, if he may have stated his case too strongly. It is an interesting question. However, what we may not ignore is the impact of Abraham's *The Logic of Evangelism* on the wider field on evangelism. Had Abraham not lifted the study of evangelism to the level of serious theological inquiry, we most likely would not have seen a new generation of scholars, such as Jackson, a reason to rejoice in itself.

30. Jackson, *Proclamation*, 278.

Therefore, whether we understand evangelism from the perspective of Abraham as initiation or from Jackson's notion of proclamation, the end remains constant: people coming to know the love of God revealed in Jesus Christ and growing deep in the soil of the kingdom, moving in real and dramatic ways toward triune God.

Chapter Four

Church Growth and Evangelism

Michael J. Gehring

More than a quarter-century ago, in his groundbreaking work *The Logic of Evangelism*, William J. Abraham addressed the dearth of critical theological engagement on the praxis of evangelism. For too long, evangelism had been dominated by works that focused on practice—how-to-manuals that attempted to equip practitioners with a set of skills for their work—and provided only cursory theological reflection. Such manuals, though helpful in empowering local churches and clergy with the work at hand, did not adequately address the theological underpinnings for the work. Abraham argued that the problem within the theological academy was so severe, so acute, that there was not a consensus on what the questions or the criteria are that govern the field. He further contended that there was not an adequate concept that sufficiently delineated the components of evangelism.

This disjunction between theology and evangelism was not accidental. To be sure, there were practical works aimed at helping congregations and pastors to engage in the work of evangelism, but there was not, by-and-large, an overwhelming sense that the work was pressing. For far too long, as Abraham noted, there was "a deep sense of ease about the survival of Christianity in the West."[1] Abraham rightly noted that there was not, at that time, sufficient intellectual or moral support or resources to warrant an academic wading into this bog.

---

1. Abraham, *Logic of Evangelism*, 4.

When many clergy, bishops, and denominational executives in the various mainline denominations did turn their attention to evangelism, too often they were motivated by the need to maintain the church as institution. When the primary emphasis becomes maintaining the institution, what is often lost is an intentional strategy for individual conversion and disciple formation. What was also, at times, sacrificed was the missional identity of the church.

The mainline Protestant churches of the last half-century often employed an evangelistic methodology that focused on getting people in the pews. We could best describe this strategy as a congregation acquiring the best pulpiteer its resources allowed, opening the doors, and waiting for the mighty rush of congregants and visitors to follow. When this strategy no longer proved sufficient, the program-driven church rose to fill the void. The assumption was that people would be attracted to the churches with the best youth activities and children's educational programs.

One of the significant problems of the program-driven churches is that too often the focus became meeting institutional needs, that is, what is worship attendance and how are we meeting the budget? Lip service on how members should go beyond the walls to engage in Christian witness was frequently given with little actual resources expended for deepening the discipleship of the congregants and equipping the parishioners to be kingdom change-agents and missionaries. This portrait of mainline congregations is cursory, but it does describe the challenges, responses, and methodologies of many mainline churches navigating changing times. It does not represent every mainline congregation of that period.[2]

The mainline denominations, therefore, have not practiced evangelism well. Instead of engaging in street-evangelism, tent or church revivals, or coffee shops or media-driven evangelism, they forfeited the terrain to other churches, allowing them the opportunity to step into the vacuum. This backing away from deliberate, intentional evangelism is especially painful on the United Methodist front when we consider that the DNA of the Methodist and Wesleyan movements was clearly missionary and evangelistic. Other mainline denominations likewise treated evangelism as a stepchild, relegating it to the fundamentalist churches—or worse, to zealots.

2. Nor am I excluding the reality that some mainline congregations still function that way.

It is important to remember the cultural matrix in which Abraham's work arose in order to evaluate wisely how his proposals represented a seismic shift in the field of evangelism. For example, we can easily grow complacent and forget the scandals that rocked the church in America toward the end of the twentieth century.[3] Unfortunately, the religious scandals continued into the twenty-first century.[4] Though the clergy as a profession enjoyed high honesty and ethics ratings as a profession in the 1980s, the numbers have fallen dramatically since.[5] Sadly, many Americans now regard the moral failings of celebrity Protestant preachers or Roman Catholic clergy as almost common. Nothing is now beyond the pale. A growing distrust and cynicism of organized religion accompanied this transition from shock to commonplace.

The Christian Church has weathered scandals before. Aimee Semple McPherson, for example, made a splash in her day.[6] However, the cumulative cost of the scandals has taken a toll. As Bryan Stone writes:

> For some, the word [evangelism] calls to mind a shameful history of forced conversions, inquisitions, fraudulent television preachers, religious wars, crusades, genocide, colonization, and the ruthless expansion of Western power throughout the world. The E-word has become a dirty word—an embarrassment to the Christian and an affront to the non-Christian.[7]

3. Jimmy Bakker and Jimmy Swaggart personified the extravagance and moral failings of electronic evangelists of the late twentieth-century. From 1984–1987, *Charlotte Observer* scrutinized Bakker and the PTL Club's fund-raising, financial practices, and other mismanagement activities. The result of the investigations eventually led to the exposure of other fraudulent behavior, including paying Jessica Hahn, a church secretary, $279,000 for her silence against her accusations that Bakker and another evangelist (John Wesley Fletcher) had drugged and raped her. Swaggart, in 1988, made the front-page headlines with a sex scandal that involved a prostitute. It is not necessary to recount all of the scandals of TV evangelists and other Christian personalities from that time, but it is important to remember the effects the scandals had on the public in terms of the trust-worthiness of religious leaders.

4. Well-known scandals include: Mark Driscoll of the 14,000 member Mars Hill Church in Seattle, Ted Haggard of the 14,000 member New Life Church in Colorado Springs, Eddie Long of the 25,000 member New Birth Missionary Baptist Church in DeKalb County, Georgia, and Bill Hybels of the 25,000 member Willow Creek Community Church in South Barrington, Illinois.

5. Swift, "Honesty and Ethics."

6. For a thorough treatment of McPherson's life, ministry, and scandals, see Blumhofer, *Aimee Semple McPherson.*

7. Stone, *Evangelism after Christendom,* 10.

Abraham's work, published in the midst of these cultural and ecclesiastical storms, was a clarion call to a church that had forgotten its ways. It was a call to a church that had left in the rear-view mirror those practices which had constituted it through the ages and fallen prey to the seductions of celebrity, wealth, ego, and power. Abraham argued that the future of the church lay not in the modern, recent past but in the ancient past, in those practices that sustained the church from its earliest beginnings.

After diagnosing the problem of the church's failure to give proper and continuous attention to the traditional components of evangelism, Abraham set out to remedy this deficiency by conceptually mapping out the theology and practice of evangelism.[8] He construed evangelism as primarily "initiation into the Kingdom of God."[9] He demonstrated why proclamation—or preaching—was not sufficient to describe all the constitutive elements of evangelism. Abraham then asked if "proclamation" does not fully represent evangelism should it instead be construed as church growth? Here, Donald McGavran and C. Peter Wagner come into play, as they are widely regarded as the founders of the Church Growth Movement. Professors at Fuller Theological Seminary's School of World Mission, McGavran and Wagner published *Understanding Church Growth* in 1970.[10] It quickly became a standard in the field of Church Growth studies as they sought to understand the dynamics of church growth utilizing a multi-disciplinary approach, employing sociological, anthropological, and psychological tools, as well as communications theory and statistical studies.

Evaluating the Church Growth Movement, Abraham takes a positive view. He acknowledges the complicated history of evangelism and the way many in the church have sought to distance themselves from its messiness. Abraham commends McGavran for his sheer tenacity to keep before the church the concerns of the Church Growth Movement. In addition, Abraham also recognizes that we all should commend the Church Growth Movement for its determination to get to the facts; that is, there is a concerted effort on the part of McGavran and Wagner to restore "pioneer

8. Abraham, who trained as an analytic philosopher at Oxford, entered into a field of studies in the 1980s heavily bent to praxis and argued for the logic of evangelism. For consideration of his work as an analytic philosopher, see Abraham, *Canon and Criterion in Christian Theology*, and the two-volume set, Abraham, *Divine Agency and Divine Action*.

9. Abraham, *Logic of Evangelism*, 13.

10. It is puzzling that Abraham does not engage with Church Growth experts of his own United Methodist tradition—such as George Hunter.

evangelism" to the church's missionary efforts and to engage with all "the complex theological issues" their work elevates.[11] Abraham illumines these complicated problems in church growth theory and practice by noting how "significant tensions exist between the requirements and character of authentic evangelism and the principles and policies of the church growth tradition."[12] A kind of fierce pragmatism reigns. Church growth research has revealed, for instance, that a majority of Americans who join a church do so not because of mass mailings or cold-call street evangelism, but due to a friendship network.[13] Abraham cautions that the dangers inherent in such a strategy turns friendship and love into one more utilitarian mechanism to increase the size of the congregation. Furthermore, such pragmatism, as Abraham contends, can lead church growth theorists to overestimate what they have in fact achieved.[14]

Another problematic aspect lurking within church growth practice is the temptation for celebrity, higher clergy salaries, and power. Pastors who fall prey to the temptations of significance and influence put in place tools and programs that emphasize numerical growth. Not all pastors who attend church growth seminars do so of their own accord. Abraham noted that some mainline denominational executives are so panicked over the numerical decline and so desperate to reverse the course that they readily reach for any "magic wand" regardless of theological ramifications.[15] Abraham cautions the church on how these forces can create "a new canon of saints and heroes whose primary credentials are their ability to produce external results."[16]

Church growth studies often tend to subordinate theology. Abraham argues that the theological considerations McGavran pursues in *Understanding Church Growth* are secondary to the growth of the church. The pragmatism inherent in the field exists not only in method but also in theory. Competing and conflicting doctrinal traditions, for instance, can utilize church growth without "shedding any theological tears."[17] We can graft church growth theory onto any approach we want (e.g., Calvinism,

11. Abraham, *Logic of Evangelism*, 75–76.

12. Abraham, *Logic of Evangelism*, 77.

13. Abraham, *Logic of Evangelism*, 77.

14. Abraham, *Logic of Evangelism*, 77.

15. Abraham, *Logic of Evangelism*, 78.

16. Abraham, *Logic of Evangelism*, 78.

17. Abraham, *Logic of Evangelism*, 80.

Dispensationalism, Pentecostalism, the psychological hedonism of Robert Schuller, or even the prosperity gospel of Robert Tilton).[18] The result is "theological disarray and shallowness," "a fostering of false hopes" of what the church can achieve by programs and research, and the painful reality that such maneuvering fails to live anywhere near the radical demands of the gospel.[19]

Since the publication of *The Logic of Evangelism*, time has demonstrated how prescient Abraham was. His criticisms of the Church Growth Movement might have struck some, when Abraham first lodged them, as being overly critical. After all, what right-thinking Christian would oppose the growth of the church? Yet, Abraham clearly saw within the Church Growth Movement temptations that would prove all too overwhelming for a church in decline—temptations that, if we follow the right methods of hospitality, marketing, and demographics, we may turn around the church. Yet getting people into a church does not necessarily correlate with forming deeply committed disciples. Willow Creek, the megachurch in Barrington, Illinois, not only engaged in a thorough analysis of their ministries but also published the results. What they discovered, as a pulpit and program-driven church, is that increased levels of participation in various activities of the church did not necessarily lead to someone becoming a more deeply committed disciple of Jesus Christ.[20]

Mainline denominations have been declining for more than a half-century. We can see on the horizon how, in less than twenty years, that these once bulwarks of the nation's religious life might cease to exist.[21] The temptation to fill the pews at all costs is great. One can understand why so many thought that church growth might provide the "magic pill."

Nevertheless, there is a dark side. The casualty count of the Church Growth Movement is in plain view as denominational executives seek more numerical results. Clergy depression and other health-related illnesses have increased over the years, and what was once one of the healthiest of the white-collar professions has seen a decline in fortune.[22] The constant pres-

18. Abraham, *Logic of Evangelism*, 81.

19. Abraham, *Logic of Evangelism*, 81.

20. Hawkins et al., *Reveal*.

21. Stetzer, "If it doesn't stem its decline, mainline Protestantism has just 23 Easters left."

22. See Proeschold-Bell and McDevitt, "Overview," and Proeschold-Bell and Le-Grand, "High Rates of Obesity."

sure to produce results has contributed to an exodus of clergy leaving the ministry.[23]

More research is also needed exploring the effects church growth theory and techniques have upon the laity. Pastors, who have attended church growth workshops at the megachurch of the moment, return, often times, to traditional churches filled with parishioners who joined the church because they like it as it is. Many congregations experienced what Thomas G. Long described as the "worship wars." Stanley Hauerwas, a lay-Methodist, theologian, and ethicist at Duke University, provides an anecdotal account of what it was like to be a parishioner in a church whose pastor wanted to make changes in order to foster church growth.[24] After the pastor returned from a church growth seminar and started to implement changes, Hauerwas vocalized his objections. She accused him of being against "evangelization." He countered that he was all for evangelization, but against employing "economic modes of life incompatible with the gospel."[25] Often times, pastors and other church leaders pitch their proposals for change wrapped up with implicit promises that if the congregation allows descending screens, loud band praise music, projection systems, and informal worship, their church will attract young people. Of course, such a pragmatic, utilitarian, and coercive strategy is difficult for older members to resist as they long for their church to have a future. Such an implied promise is one that no one can guarantee as the millennial generation continues to demonstrate a less-than-significant interest in the institutional church.

The differences between protestant megachurches and megachurches of other traditions needs further study as well. In the video link accompanying the story "Lessons on Evangelization from the Largest Parish in the United States," John J. McSweeney, then pastor of St. Matthew Roman Catholic Church in Charlotte, North Carolina, shared the impressions his congregants had from visiting other congregations. As St. Matthew began to experience explosive growth, it sent out teams to some of America's well-known megachurches to learn the best practices, and what became clear is that, too often, the star is the pastor. McSweeney stated that, at St. Matthew's, the star is Jesus Christ.[26]

---

23. For a helpful resource, see Hoge and Wenger, *Pastors in Transition*.

24. Hauerwas, *Hannah's Child*, 221, 258, 259.

25. Hauerwas, *Hannah's Child*, 259.

26. Libresco, "Lessons on Evangelization."

St. Matthew has more than 10,000 registered households in its congregation, and weekend worship attendance ranges from 10,000 to 12,000. An interesting research project would be to consider how megachurches that are more focused on the Eucharist (such as from the Roman Catholic and the Orthodox traditions) compare against the Protestant megachurches (often times driven more by the senior pastor's charisma and pulpit presence) in the transition of senior pastors. McSweeney retired on July 18, 2017, and, though St. Matthew's will certainly have some bumps in the road with the transition of senior pastors, it will not experience the significant turbulence that many megachurches encounter.

The Crystal Cathedral provides an example of a very unsuccessful transition of senior pastors at a megachurch. For many years, the Crystal Cathedral served as a training ground for potential megachurch pastors with the Robert H. Schuller Institute for Successful Church Leadership. The transition from the founding pastor, Robert H. Schuller, to his son, Robert A. Schuller, failed to bring about the desired future. What followed was a series of financial and leadership crises, infighting in the Schuller family, and eventually a bankruptcy judge selling the Crystal Cathedral property to the Roman Catholic Diocese of Orange County. It was an ignominious end to Schuller's positive possibility thinking gospel.

What time has demonstrated since the publication of *The Logic of Evangelism* is that the problems Abraham diagnosed have only become more acute. Mainline Protestantism has not adequately addressed the crisis of initiation and formation. My own denomination, the United Methodist Church, still does not have an official catechism nor a mandatory catechesis process. New church members and those who have been in the pews for decades are ill-equipped to deal with the moralistic, therapeutic deism of our age, with the seduction by materialism, the conflict between nationalism and the kingdom of God, and a host of other ever-present dangers.

Abraham was right not only to address the problems inherent to the Church Growth Movement but also to commend it for the good it has accomplished. The Church Growth Movement is an extremely important development, and the challenge is how to integrate it into the life of the church without allowing it to corrupt the church. The star in our churches must always be Jesus. The problem of accommodation continually presents temptations for the church: temptations to bend the knee to pragmatism and to allow results to be our god, temptations to tolerate theological ambiguity, temptations for syncretism, temptations to short-sell proper initiation for the expediency of the moment, and temptations to turn our institutions into golden calves. In a letter to the editor of *The Church Times*, C.S. Lewis wrote that what unites the Evangelical and the Anglo-Catholic against the "Liberal" or "Modernist" is that both are "thoroughgoing supernaturalists."[27] Lewis argued that the terms "Low" church or "High" church fail to adequately describe what is at stake, offering "Deep Church" as an alternative.[28] In the midst of crumbling institutions, now is the time for the church to resist simply growing broader and instead grow deeper in wisdom and truth.

27. Lewis, *Narnia, Cambridge, and Joy*, 164.
28. Lewis, *Narnia, Cambridge, and Joy*, 164.

Chapter Five

Evangelism as Initiation

ANDREW D. KINSEY

CENTRAL TO WILLIAM ABRAHAM'S *The Logic of Evangelism* is the claim that we can improve our thinking on evangelism by conceiving of it as "that set of intentional activities which is governed by the goal of initiating people into the kingdom of God for the first time."[1] Contrasting this conception of evangelism with church growth and proclamation, not to mention witness, soul-winning, and discipleship, Abraham elucidates the key reasons why the church needs to implement this vision of evangelism while also addressing objections others may render about it. The primary ingredient Abraham wants readers to swallow is the way evangelism as initiation avoids reductionism on the one hand while understanding evangelism as a complex "web of reality" on the other—a web of reality that is at once "corporate, cognitive, moral, experienced, operational, and disciplinary," neither reducible to one thing nor all strung together by mere human effort.[2] No, evangelism is "all of these activities set and bounded within the dramatic action of God that is manifest in Christ and fueled by the Holy Spirit."[3] This change of focus from the anthropocentric to the theocentric is how evangelism as initiation can move more coherently into the future.[4]

Abraham's contribution in *The Logic of Evangelism*, therefore, is to reorient evangelism toward initiation into God's kingdom. While others in

1. Abraham, *Logic of Evangelism*, 95.
2. Abraham, *Logic of Evangelism*, 96.
3. Abraham, *Logic of Evangelism*, 103.
4. Abraham, *Logic of Evangelism*, 98, 113.

this volume have aptly mentioned this concept (as it is the central piece of Abraham's overall argument), we will want to remember how Abraham sets out to counter objections to what he is proposing.[5] The reason that we want to keep in mind such objections is to realize that Abraham's project wants to keep in place the overall goal or *teleos* to the practice of evangelism: the rule or reign of God's kingdom. This insight is significant because Abraham makes it clear that evangelism—indeed, ministry as whole in the life of the church—must take into account the grand sweep of God's agency in history.[6] The power of God's rule in Jesus of Nazareth through the activity of the Holy Spirit provides the theological horsepower to the various dimensions or activities of initiation. In other words, according to Abraham, *logically* prior to initiation or incorporation into the church is the rule or activity of God and what God has done in Christ; the primary horizon is theological, not anthropocentric.[7] It is the awesome actions of the triune God that establishes this vision of evangelism. Without such divine agency, the scaffolding of the house of evangelism crumbles.[8]

Such theological hairsplitting may prove off-putting to some, and yet, in light of Scott Jones's work on evangelism, the relation of God's kingdom to the church in the ministry of evangelism is critical to the way we may conceive of evangelism.[9] Jones's argument builds on Abraham's approach throughout his *The Evangelistic Love of God & Neighbor*, and like Abraham, conceives of evangelism as initiation. Jones agrees with Abraham on many points, adding and clarifying as he proposes an approach to evangelism in terms of initiation into Christian discipleship as a response to God's reign.[10] Jones's critique of Abraham is conceptual, noting how Abraham's definition of evangelism as initiation into God's kingdom makes God's kingdom no wider than the ministry of the church. Indeed, there is confusion over where the kingdom and church are in Abraham's conceptual scheme.[11] This criticism may have stuck as Jones comments on how Abraham addresses this insight ten years later.[12] What is clear to Jones is that the argument

---

5. See, in particular, the chapters by Jones and Meadows in this volume.

6. Abraham, *Logic of Evangelism*, 101.

7. Abraham, *Logic of Evangelism*, 98, 114.

8. Abraham, *Logic of Evangelism*, 98.

9. See Jones, *Evangelistic Love*, especially 68–73.

10. Jones, *Evangelistic Love*, 73.

11. Jones, *Evangelistic Love*, 70.

12. Abraham, "On Making Disciples," 150–66.

Abraham proffered with respect to the primary actors in evangelism in *The Logic of Evangelism* in 1989 remains a topic of ongoing reflection today: that though the primary agent in evangelism is the triune God, there is also the church, the evangelist, and the person and/or persons evangelized.[13] The interaction and relationship of all these actors constitute a robust "web of reality." A host of philosophical and theological issues are in play. Therefore, whether conceived as initiation into God's reign for the first time (Abraham) or as initiation into Christian discipleship in response to God's reign (Jones), the agency of God in the work of evangelism and in the fields of practical and systematic theology continues to spark much needed conversation.[14]

I interject Scott Jones's work at this point to highlight a central feature of Abraham's notion of evangelism as initiation: while geared theologically toward the inbreaking of God's rule in Jesus Christ by workings of the Holy Spirit, the practice of evangelism remains, and very much is, a polymorphous activity, much akin to farming or education.[15] There is simply no way of separating the human elements from the divine initiatives with respect to catechesis and preaching, or moral and spiritual formation, not to mention witnessing and discipleship.[16] To be considered evangelism, however, all of these dimensions must somehow be causally related to the process of initiation into God's rule—that is, governed by the intention to achieve this particular end or goal.[17]

I make this assertion because a critical aspect of Abraham's approach to evangelism is how it is not some ahistorical process. Rather, as Abraham notes, evangelism has a definite social and communal character, one grounded in the very community or people of Israel.[18] Evangelism rubs shoulders with least, the last, and the lost, and sits in the smoking section

---

13. Abraham, *Logic of Evangelism*, 103–4.

14. Abraham makes reference to this conversation in Abraham, *Crossing the Threshold*, 172. However, in the field of practical theology, Andrew Root has raised instructive questions regarding the importance of God's active presence and agency. Too many practical theologians, according to Root, have failed to give account of the ways in which God works to save, heal, and redeem, relying instead on descriptive accounts of material conditions to what is happening. See Root, *Christopraxis*, 79.

15. Abraham, *Logic of Evangelism*, 104.

16. See the chapters by Wende and Moreau in this volume for insights into the various dimensions of initiation.

17. Abraham, *Logic of Evangelism*, 105.

18. Abraham, *Logic of Evangelism*, 102.

of the hotel, if not rides the back of the bus.[19] In other words, Abraham's notion of evangelism is very much incarnational. It includes the affections and dispositions of all human beings, with various historical and cultural realities, always contending with the reality of God's intentions and purposes.[20] Abraham makes this point apparent when he cites the example of the Prophet Harris of the Ivory Coast. Harris's commitment to evangelism was simple and to the point, a ministry marked by various activities from building houses to keeping the sabbath. It was a ministry that in many respects carried out numerous dimensions of evangelism. And yet, in light of Abraham's vision of evangelism, may not fully measure up.[21]

Not to fret! To implement Abraham's vision of evangelism is to understand the very messiness of history—anomalies in history do not serve as warrants to discount fundamental principles with regards to the conception of evangelism as initiation.[22] In other words, what we need in the ministry of evangelism, indeed, in the wider mission of the church, is the cultivation of a kind of sensitivity with respect to cultural and social contexts where our evangelistic endeavors take shape, as well as the kind of rigorous theological reflection to support such endeavors. We do not need to throw out the proverbial theological baby with the contextual bathwater. Rather, our endeavors need to seek an ultimate endpoint. To paraphrase a quip of G.K. Chesterton, we should not discount the notion of evangelism as initiation because it has not been tried and found wanting; we should realize that it has been found difficult and not tried, especially throughout the history of the church and on the mission field. The eschatological reign of God does not preclude thoughtful action in the present but rather draws it forth into critical dialogue toward a new future, wherever we may serve in God's redemptive mission. Therefore, that we would dismiss Prophet Harris's attempts in evangelism as falling short of Abraham's vision and view it as wrongheaded is shortsighted; it is not. Equally, that we would discount the principles upon which we would implement evangelism as initiation into God's rule is empty; such ministry or mission endeavors as Harris's do not dismiss such proposals. Rather, we bring both aspects of our theological

19. Abraham, *Logic of Evangelism*, 102, 106. See also Abraham's chapter "Dying for Renewal" in Abraham, *Logic of Renewal* where he cites Oscar Romero and Martin Luther King as examples of those whose ministries embodied the logic of the gospel's power to influence society.

20. Abraham, *Logic of Evangelism*, 102.

21. Abraham, *Logic of Evangelism*, 105.

22. Abraham, *Logic of Evangelism*, 106.

and missional endeavors under the guidance of the Holy Spirit and proceed with trusting awareness and obedience.

Needless to say, Abraham foresees such possible objections to this approach to evangelism, whether from the whole "quantity versus quality" debate—a bogus contrast—to the way evangelism as initiation may confuse evangelism with other ministries in the church, like Christian education and nurture.[23] Abraham's point is not to squash these objections outright but rather to keep our wits about us in ways that can provide helpful distinctions. The task is to note the importance of fundamental theological foundations in how we carry out ministry. Accordingly, the church can proceed with initiation with integrity (e.g., addressing the misunderstanding of the notion of overloading new converts with the imposing demands of God's rule).[24] Abraham is keenly aware of how the form and content of the gospel must take center stage in the initiation process rather than look for greener grass on the other side of the fence, sensing the new convert cannot handle the commitment and jettison the whole process.[25] We need not worry. We need not out of fear reduce the overarching goal of evangelism as initiation into a stuffy lecture (a misleading notion) or so complicate it as to never get it off the ground (a way to beg the question). There are no microwavable solutions. Instead, the governing goal is to envision evangelism as a multisided activity grounded in God's living rule in Christ, clarifying distinctions along the way, but always insisting on the logical primacy of the kingdom and always with patience and pastoral sensitivity.[26] Heart and mind are not in contention but rather in wakeful awareness of God's prior work.[27]

Such objections, however, do not exhaust what others in the field of evangelism have registered about Abraham's conception of evangelism. Notable is Elaine Robinson. She criticizes Abraham's arguments about evangelism as initiation as focusing the conversation too narrowly on what she

23. Abraham, *Logic of Evangelism*, 108.

24. Abraham, *Logic of Evangelism*, 109.

25. Abraham, *Logic of Evangelism*, 110.

26. Abraham, *Logic of Evangelism*, 106.

27. Abraham begins his chapter on initiation with a helpful recapitulation of the history of the divergent approaches to initiation and to the ways the church has typically narrowed the focus of God's activity. Too often the church has failed to see how initiation into the kingdom of God will have its own internal grammar, structure, constraints, and logic. It is one of the many reasons the church remains confused on matters of evangelism and on the ways of understanding God's agency in shaping new followers in the faith. See Abraham, *Logic of Evangelism*, 96–97.

understands *Evangelicalism* has become in the contemporary sense.[28] Apparently, Abraham's approach to evangelism as initiation would not appeal to the large numbers of Christians who do not share views many Evangelicals hold, such as church growth, conversion, and substitutionary atonement (to name three).[29] Though she makes helpful distinctions between Evangelicalism and evangelism, she lumps Abraham and his proposals into the "evangelical camp," proffering reasons why many Christians should not give credence to his arguments—reasons, unbeknownst to Abraham, that posit the following: 1) his "white, male, middle-class perspective" is really a camouflage to universal domination, 2) he uses scripture selectively, 3) he defines evangelism in ways that promote the status quo rather than challenging it, and 4) he displays triumphalist tendencies.[30] It is not clear Robinson has fully digested *The Logic of Evangelism*, but the objections she raises brings to the surface several issues with respect to theological method and to the assumptions she holds of a large movement within the church (i.e., Evangelicalism), not to mention Abraham's own position.[31]

Therefore, it is difficult to know where to begin with Robinson's characterization of Abraham's proposals. The blind spots one readily sees in someone else's position has the tendency to reveal the logs in one's own (Matt 7:3–5). Shibboleths usually do not withstand critical scrutiny. It is why, without falling into "strawmen" polemics, we want to remain clear as

---

28. See Robinson, *Godbearing*, 41–44.

29. Robinson, *Godbearing*, 44. Robinson utilizes the work of David Bebbington and Mark Noll to delineate the tenets or beliefs of Evangelicalism. As a movement within the church catholic, Evangelicalism is hardly monolithic, but it constitutes a large and varied and always changing kaleidoscope of colors and figures. Interestingly, Robinson does not mention other tributaries within the broader movement (e.g., Pietist, Pentecostal, Holiness, Wesleyan). Such tributaries, of course, do not easily settle into the fixed categories Robinson indicates.

30. Robinson, *Godbearing*, 44. Abraham does offer a severe critique of Evangelicalism (Abraham, *Logic of Evangelism*, 199). However, it is not clear why Robinson fails to register it or track where Abraham goes with affirming a classical expression of the gospel. Apparently, these concerns fall outside her purview.

31. Abraham's position is not always easy to capture, especially within the larger currents of Evangelicalism. Abraham's project of canonical theism, for example, while compatible with aspects of Evangelicalism, would make some Evangelicals nervous, such as the way he navigates the various theories of the divine inspiration of scripture. See, in particular, Abraham, *Coming Great Revival*. Simply placing Abraham in the Evangelical camp does not do justice to the finer distinctions in play in the field of evangelism that Abraham puts forth nor to his own theological contribution; see Abraham et al., *Canonical Theism*, especially chapter 1.

to what is before us, especially with respect to this volume of essays: that first, since the publication of *The Logic of Evangelism*, the *status quo* of both church and academy has been altered, if not changed, with regards to the way we conceive of evangelism and the ministry of evangelism as initiation. Intellectual honesty requires this recognition. Persons in the field of evangelism must deal with the issues Abraham's work raises. There is no going back to reductionist accounts of evangelism.[32] Second, *contra* Robinson, Abraham's use of scripture remains consistent throughout his work and on par with the longstanding work in biblical scholarship, especially the New Testament. If anything, Abraham's proposals at the beginning of *The Logic of Evangelism* call for greater conversation between the two fields, not less, and bring to light the *whole* nature of the biblical canon, not selective aspects of it. Abraham's proposals actually operate to foster greater mutual respect—if not ongoing clarification—between biblical studies and evangelistic efforts.[33] Third, careful reading of *The Logic of Evangelism*, while a strain to some, reveals that the triumphalistic tendency under negotiation is the triumph of the gospel. There is, according to Abraham, actually a gospel to proclaim with form and content in the face of sin and death! That later in *The Logic of Evangelism*, Abraham would utilize the notion of winning souls into the kingdom, and that this language would prescribe a form of triumphalism, promoting an "us versus them" mindset, then, is a stretch.[34] Viewed within Abraham's overall set of proposals "winning" actually describes a form of threshold crossing or the way in which God acts within us to shape us into followers of Jesus Christ as grateful and faithful servants. Hardly triumphalistic![35]

32. See Abraham, "Theology of Evangelism," 128–29.

33. A careful reading of chapter 2 in *Logic of Evangelism* demonstrates the dialogue with which Abraham is engaged with respect to biblical scholarship, rightly noting the profound tension between the "already" and "not yet" character of God's kingdom (Abraham, *Logic of Evangelism*, 23–32). Robinson's focus on the "eschatological" in Abraham's approach fails to take note of these distinctions. See Robison, *Godbearing*, 51.

34. Abraham's argument on winning persons to the Christian faith needs to be placed in the context of his chapter on "Wider Ecumenism," where he aptly proposes how evangelists may respect the freedom of others and yet remained committed to the gospel. Within the Christian tradition itself, there are constraints that provide such instruction, not to mention the virtues of patience and humility (Abraham, *Logic of Evangelism*, 229). Robinson's selective use of Abraham's position does not do justice to the overall thrust of Abraham's framework. See Robinson, *Godbearing*, 57.

35. See Abraham, *Logic of Evangelism*, 212, 229. It is interesting to note how Abraham's argument with respect to a "high Christology" does not automatically lead to the

And fourth, to dismiss Abraham's theological contributions to the field of evangelism on the basis of his race and gender simply begs the questions under consideration and reveals the "dark cave" into which so much of "mainline" Protestant theology has descended.[36] To discount Abraham's ecclesiology as "hierarchical" or "high church" because he advocates the classical creeds, the historical episcopate, or the basic canon of scripture, and seeks to establish the patristic period as normative only illumines the basic lack of agreement in the criteria by which we now carry out theology in fulfilling the church's mission.[37] Robinson's comment that Abraham fails to take seriously the Protestant Reformation or the priesthood of all believers, in addition, only confuses the issue at hand and raises more suspicion: how is it that in our attempts to demonstrate value to "specific contexts" or "concrete persons" (i.e., a person's affections, gender, race, customs, traditions, etc.) we can so readily turn around and reject out of hand other historical contexts or persons, simply on a notion that such contexts and persons represent "hierarchy," which now has become synonymous with oppression? Privileging the Protestant Reformation, or any other period of history of course, comes with its own risks and dangers. If anything, it only compounds the problem. After all, we may also read the Reformation as an attempt to recapture the sources of the patristic period for the renewal of

---

kind of imperial practices Robinson maintains. Rather, as Abraham's example of the Moravian missionaries in the West Indies indicates, a "high Christology" can also lead to radical forms of service and witness (Abraham, *Logic of Evangelism*, 221). See also Abraham, *Crossing the Threshold*, 110–12.

36. I use the image of the "deep cave" from Mark Lilla's *Once and Future Liberal*, where he critiques "liberals" who have succumbed to the politics of identity, staying within their own little caves, and not coming out to find ways of sharing in the common life of the nation (Lilla, *Once and Future Liberal*, 9–10). I am suggesting similar forces are at work within the "mainline" Protestant churches where theology has become more identified with partisan affiliation than with the "faith once delivered to the saints" (Titus 2).

37. Abraham addresses the issues of criteria in theology in Abraham, *Canon and Criterion*, especially in the chapter, "Theological Foundationalism," as well as the opening chapter, "Orientation." These two chapters place the issues that Robinson's argument raises in a larger historical and theological horizon. In addition, the notion of a "high Christology" does not necessarily rule out approaches to church "from below." For example, Abraham cites how John Wesley's own missionary endeavors usually began from the "bottom up," walking a fine line between institution and community. Wesley's reliance on the Holy Spirit at ground level was critical to uniting other believers to Christ, rich and poor. See Abraham, *Wesley for Armchair Theologians*, 120.

the church, not to mention a return to the whole of scripture! The Protestant Reformation was hardly monolithic.[38]

We highlight these objections to Robinson's argument not as a way to congratulate ourselves but as a way to intensify our work in the field of evangelism and to realize how Abraham's notion of evangelism as initiation into the kingdom of God in the life of the church is highly compatible with a view or an "ecclesiology from below"; that what we see in Abraham's approach to evangelism is how evangelists, ministers, and missionaries in the trenches can bring to the fore a whole host of treasures from the church's rich theological heritage—not to mention insights from social philosophy and theory—to announce the glad tidings of salvation. If anything, what we realize in Abraham's work is how it can foster greater use of such resources on the ground, deploying them as guided by the Holy Spirit in the concrete situations of mission and life, serving as priests to God's gracious rule. Gladly, there are furnishings within the church's household that can provide such sustenance.[39]

We offer these insights as a way to continue the conversation about evangelism in the life of the church knowing, as our above midrash on Robinson's objections makes clear, we are very much in the arena of dealing with essentially contested concepts.[40] Whether we are distinguishing between Evangelicalism and evangelism, or classical orthodoxy and liberationist theologies, we stand in constant need of clarification, if not qualification, about our claims. Honesty requires such acumen. And yet, such an insight is not new. What is new, and where Abraham's work instructively points,

38. The celebration of the 500th Anniversary of Protestant Reformation unleashed a tidal wave of responses as to what Luther's actions have meant to the church. Clearly, there was more than one Reformation (e.g., the Roman Catholic Counter-Reformation, the Swiss Reformation, the English Reformation, to name three). In play were a wide variety of issues, one of which was coming to grips with what counts as normative in the Christian life (e.g., the role of scripture, creeds, confessions, etc.), Abraham's project, far from constituting a "high ecclesiology," is really a search for the theological treasures that may bring healing to the church's divisions. See, in particular, Abraham, *Canonical Theism*, 303.

39. In *Logic of Evangelism*, Abraham notes the profoundly intergenerational nature to the ministry of initiation as a way to pass on the treasures of the church. Therefore, contrary to Robinson, who sees Abraham's position as taking human beings out of history, especially among the oppressed, Abraham's intergenerational approach to evangelism and ministry actually operates to keep us grounded in actual human realities, always seeking to find our way home to God, but never forgetting our neighbors. The Christian tradition is rich in such moral and theological treasures, 114–15.

40. See Gallie, "Essentially Contested Concepts," 155.

is how we may proceed within contested traditions and have the epistemic humility to say so.[41] It is one of the reasons we need not only to stay abreast of the happenings within the discipline of theology but also to understand the deep reservoirs of orthodox faith and practice.[42] Such a stance is actually healthy as it can promote theological vitality, especially on the mission field where we practice discipleship. Indeed, it is the shepherd-evangelist who knows how to bring to bear on the work of mission the great deposit of the faith, discerning with the sensitive disposition of heart the way the church may proceed in faithful service to the kingdom, initiating and instructing the sheep into the fold.[43] The many sides to these evangelistic-pastoral tasks are not mutually exclusive but reinforcing, governed always by the goal of initiating persons into God's rule in history.[44]

Therefore, contrary to objections that Abraham's arguments may crowd out voices around the table, the opposite is actually the case: that Abraham's proposals actually function in ways that expand the porch and deepen the conversation, if not raising the stakes; that, building on John Wesley's view of the house as holiness, we need to take seriously how we rebuild and enlarge the porch of repentance with respect to the ministry of evangelism; and that we need to figure out and understand how we may bring together all the various dimensions of initiation into a coherent framework to announce God's kingdom in every time and place, calling persons to turn to God and begin the journey of heart and mind into the Christian life. To be sure, we cannot reduce such an announcement to sensational advertising techniques and the full claims of the gospels to pithy slogans. Rather, we need to be prepared to comprehend what remains to be implemented with great care and patience: that practicing the measures and processes of initiation into God's kingdom requires a kind of perseverance

41. See, in particular, Richard Mouw's wonderful little volume, *Called to a Life of the Mind*. Mouw's notion of epistemic humility is helpful and wise (Mouw, *Called to a Life of the Mind*, 26).

42. Andrew Walker and Robin Parry aptly call attention to C. S. Lewis's notion of "Deep Church" and the way such a notion may assist the church in capturing the full force of the church's canonical treasures and practices. See Walker and Parry, *Deep Church Rising*, 49–50, and Walker, "Foreword," xii.

43. Abraham, *Logic of Evangelism*, 106.

44. Abraham rightfully mentions the lists of pastor-evangelists in the church's long history who not only gave wise counsel to those who were seeking but also worked thoughtfully to usher persons into God's kingdom. If anything, Abraham's proposals rightly lend themselves to the church's ministry of spiritual direction and pastoral care. See Abraham, *Logic of Evangelism*, 102, 113.

and that one of the greatest shortfalls to life in the kingdom would be not to find such measures and processes out of reach and too demanding but rather to fail to practice such measures and processes at all.[45]

45. Abraham, *Logic of Evangelism*, 106, 111.

Chapter Six

Conversion, Baptism, and Morality

Karin L. Wende

Introduction

I FIRST ENCOUNTERED WILLIAM J. Abraham in the spring of 1985, when he was the guest preacher for the annual conference sessions of the Southwest Texas Conference of the United Methodist Church. There is one phrase from those sermons that remains with me to this day, "I am an unrepentant supernaturalist." His steadfast insistence on the intellectual validity and personal accessibility of the supernatural has encouraged and guided the theological journeys of many of his students, including me.

Looking back to the earliest evangelists in the New Testament, Abraham notes that the theological horizon in which Jesus and his followers practiced evangelism was the kingdom or reign of God. For Abraham, the early Church's understanding of the kingdom was not merely as a doctrine about how God would eventually bring human history to its conclusion; rather, the kingdom was a powerful, transcendent reality which had come to the earth through Jesus. The kingdom was signified openly in exorcisms and miracles. It was revealed in the lives of the earliest Christians through the influence of the Holy Spirit. It was simply the supernatural realm of God, containing in itself past, present, and eschatological future, impinging on the here and now. Those disciples who had experienced the kingdom through Jesus passed on to their followers information about what the kingdom was like and what it took to enter into it personally. In fact, the communication of this information about the kingdom come-near-in Jesus was the primary task of those first followers: apostles and evangelists

*what you has done +
is doing.*

who were sent to bring the Kingdom near to the lives of as many people as possible.

Given its significance for the evangelistic efforts of the first Christians, Abraham located the modern study of evangelism solidly within the same theological horizon. Evangelism was defined as a set of practices aimed at initiating newcomers into that Kingdom for the first time.[1] Abraham argued that by restoring a proper Kingdom horizon to evangelism, the church could correct current evangelistic reflection and practice might enrich the ministry of evangelism. *The Logic of Evangelism* was, in a very basic sense, a demonstration of how such an approach would work. For example, although most 1989 approaches to evangelism gave a nod to God, much of the focus was on human agency. Abraham's new perspective clearly identified evangelism's primary agent as God. This was not to say that humans do not participate in this endeavor but rather that God's role is primary.[2] The focus of evangelism, therefore, is always on what God has already done in Christ and what he continues to do in specific situations. The faithful evangelist is someone who operates out of an informed understanding of the reign of God, including an awareness of God's transcendent presence in the here and now. To do faithful evangelism within this theological horizon is first to look for how the reign of God is manifest in a given situation so as to cooperate with what God was already doing. Abraham's new definition of evangelism also broadened the goal of evangelism. Initiation into the reign of God is a far more profound purpose than Church membership, congregational growth, the remediation of social ills, or even the assurance of an eventual arrival in heaven for the convert. The evangelized are to enter into a present-tense transformational relationship with God.

The implications of Abraham's focus on the reign of God extended to the church as well. For Abraham, the fact that the reign was the theological horizon of the early church pointed to the need for the contemporary church to refocus on it. Outside of the reign of God, there is no reason for the church to exist. "The kingdom of God must be the primary, unconditional priority of the Church, which exists in and for the coming of the rule of God in history. Only as she exists in and for that kingdom is she authentic and valid."[3] This position is not to deny the existence of the kingdom

1. Abraham, *Logic of Evangelism*, 95.

2. Abraham, *Logic of Evangelism*, 33, 103, 168. Abraham actually named four agents in evangelism: God, the Church, the evangelist, and the potential convert.

3 Abraham, *Logic of Evangelism*, 182.

in other contexts. Abraham was clear that salvation through Christ as the eternal Son, not expressly identified as the historical Jesus, is a clear potential.[4] Abraham's position did insist, however, that the church which does not operate out of a here-and-now experience of the kingdom is not valid. Insofar as the church exists for the kingdom, it has a mandate to "embody the rule of God in its worship, life and ministries."[5] As participant in the kingdom, the church is gifted with divine power to accomplish its tasks. "There is no denying that the Holy Spirit was experienced [in the early church] as a dynamic agent of the rule of God empowering and equipping the church to act an agent of the kingdom in the present."[6] As an embodiment of the reign of God, it serves as a place or community in which that Kingdom becomes accessible to the world.

Abraham developed his approach by identifying six dimensions to evangelism which together captured an understanding of evangelism within the horizon of the reign of God: corporate, cognitive, moral, experiential, operational, and disciplinary qualities. The church is to consider these dimensions—not just separately but rather with a view to grasping how all six work together. Attending to all six dimensions in order to faithfully conduct God's new children into their new home in the kingdom is properly the responsibility of the church, empowered by the charisms of the Holy Spirit. Abraham explored in some detail conversion (an aspect of the experiential dimension), baptism (initiation into the corporate body of the church), and morality (the moral dimension) in chapter six. The other three are addressed in chapter seven.

Abraham began his discussion of conversion in chapter six with an illustration, citing Thomas Carlyle's description of a lackluster church which had become little more than a cultural appendage. Carlyle set the empty, powerless members of that church in contrast to the vitality of those who had experienced a transforming encounter with Christ. Abraham, while affirming the need for such an encounter, argued that Carlyle's position was incomplete. Placing conversion within the horizon of the reign of God provided a more comprehensive theological framework and guarded against some of the erroneous and unproductive practices which had emerged by the time of *The Logic of Evangelism's* composition. Like Carlyle, Abraham defined conversion as the new birth or transformation which takes

---

4. Abraham, *Logic of Evangelism*, 220.

5. Abraham, *Logic of Evangelism*, 103.

6. Abraham, *Logic of Evangelism*, 103.

place when a person, confronted and convicted by the Holy Spirit, accepts Christ's offer to enter into God's reign. The new convert is acquitted, assured, and brought into a new relationship with God. However, the situation in 1989 demonstrated how, even when this language was employed, the church could lose its moorings. This description of conversion had become confined to a "theological underworld"[7] in which it was divorced from other dimensions of evangelism. Taking conversion to be the product of a personal divine encounter—without serious consideration of its place or purpose in the reign of God—had produced a series of corrupt and/ or distorted beliefs and practices. Instead of a consistent and unwavering focus on God's kingdom, many of those who had been converted became distracted by the self, the economy, superficial moralism, or politics. Like the members of Carlyle's representative church, they had developed into little more than appendages of culture.

The misuse of conversion language to serve less than kingdom purposes gave rise to a number of reactive movements, including the various liberation theologies. In his discussion of conversion, Abraham engaged the work of José Míguez Bonino. Bonino had argued that Wesley's assumptions about being and doing require a re-visitation of his concept of conversion because being and doing are much more intimately connected than Wesley understood. An individual does not simply experience an internal change and then act out of that new ontology. Instead, interior and exterior experiences are intertwined such that the activities and experiences of the physical body also affect one's internal perspectives.[8] Bonino's concern was that evangelism must always take into account the relational and physical context in which potential converts are found. Abraham affirmed Bonino's insight, pointing to historical Wesleyan involvement with social issues. The concerns of social injustice are very much part of the moral content of the reign of God. However, Abraham also warned about the danger of substituting, like those in the "theological underworld" above, an exclusive emphasis on liberation theology for the fullness of the kingdom.

Using Bonino's observation about the role that communities play in the formation of its members, Abraham moved to the role of the church in the formation of converts, focusing on baptism in chapter six. Abraham's

---

7. Abraham, *Logic of Evangelism*, 122.

8. Zajonc, "Emotion and Facial Efference," 15–21. Bonino's observation has been substantiated even on a smaller scale. Zajonc's study demonstrates that a subject's mood is improved simply by forcing a smile. See also Markham, *Rewired*.

discussion of baptism was closely determined by his conception of the Church as locus for the kingdom on earth. As the church fulfils its calling to live both in and for the kingdom, it is a community that participates in two realities. It is fully present in the here and now, ministering to the world and its own people as an agent of God. It is also present in the eschatological future, where God's will is to be completely accomplished. Baptism is the means by which converts enter the Church and become part of this community which has its life both in the here and now as well as the there-and-then. Given the dual loci of the Church, Baptism is both a rite performed by humans and a transforming work of God. The Church's earthly role in baptism is to provide present-tense sustenance, support, and community before and after baptism for those who would enter and remain within the reign of God. The earthly church performs the rituals and rites which make the baptismal candidate aware of and vulnerable to the Holy Spirit. As participant in the eschatological reign of God, the church also receives as a gift the power to effectively call upon the Holy Spirit in baptism.[9] In baptism, newcomers who have said yes to God are transformed by being joined, in eschatological time, to Christ in his atoning death and resurrection and entering, like the church, into the present and future kingdom.

Abraham's position is based on the baptismal theology and practices of the early Church, which as a rule, baptized adults.[10] This position is consistent within his evangelistic focus, which also, as a rule, involves adults. Infant baptism, in Abraham's view, was one of several practices which had resulted in the separation of baptism from the other aspects of Christian initiation. Abraham considered this separation a theological scandal. Insofar as the goal of evangelism is a cognizant entry into the kingdom of a co-operative convert, without baptism, the entry point is lost. The new convert is ushered into an earthly Church community, but not provided ecclesial access to the Holy Spirit and the reign of God.[11] The newcomer does not

---

9. Abraham, *Logic of Evangelism*, 157n17.

10. See, for example Cyril, *Works*; Ambrose, "On the Mysteries," 317–25; Chrysostom, *Baptismal Instructions*; Mingana, *Commentary of Theodore of Mopsuestia*. Porter and Cross, *Dimensions of Baptism* contains several recent studies on infant baptism in antiquity. Ferguson, *Baptism in the Early Church*, 856–57, maintains that infant baptism was not practiced before the end of the second century and may have emerged as an emergency measure for dying children. Abraham, *Logic of Evangelism* does not discuss the issue of the nurture or Christian formation of children.

11. Iyadurai, *Transformative Religious Experience*. This is an intriguing survey of Indian converts to Christianity, many of whom had transformational encounters with Christ before they were exposed to the Christian Church.

receive the Church's help in crossing into the kingdom, encountering the Holy Spirit, and becoming new. Abraham noted that baptism is so important to the process of initiation that, in those Christian traditions in which it has been separated from evangelism, substitute or quasi-sacramental rituals have appeared.

The final section of chapter six deals with the moral dimension of evangelism understood in light of the kingdom. Abraham selected the familiar passage from Mark 12 on the Great Commandment because of its explicit association with the kingdom. The man who honored the Great Commandment was "not far from the kingdom" (Mark 12:34). This passage indicates that the kingdom has a specific moral structure based on active love, reflecting the character of the God who rules it. It is impossible to enter the kingdom while repudiating its moral content because one cannot actively reject and serve God at the same time. In order to enter God's kingdom, a convert must consent to allow God to be king, including obedience to his moral standards. This observation is underscored by the fact that the transformation implicit in conversion and baptism is becoming like God. "For as many of you as were baptized into Christ have put on Christ" (Gal 3:27). In baptism, newcomers to the faith die to their old self-love, rising to a new life in the love of Christ.[12]

Abraham's discussion of Christian morality identified common misperceptions about it. Faithfulness to the moral requirements of the Kingdom is not solely the product of individual effort. Even with the cooperation of the Christian, fidelity to the great commandment is made possible through the transformation of conversion and baptism. Because obedience to the reign is a gift of the Holy Spirit, there is no sense in which such obedience can serve as an entry ticket. The neophyte is instead drawn into the kingdom through being "intellectually and spiritually won over by its intrinsic beauty and treasure."[13] Like all of the dimensions of evangelism, Abraham pointed out that consideration of the moral structure of the kingdom is to be set within the complex understanding of evangelism as a whole. It is not productive to make distinctions between external moral conduct, internal experience of God, and/or participation in the rites of the church. All of these dimensions are a necessary part of coming to Christ.

Abraham closed his discussion of morality with the concern that the difficulty and complexity of following the Great Commandment in daily

12. Abraham, *Logic of Evangelism*, 136.

13. Abraham, *Logic of Evangelism*, 135.

life should be taken very seriously. Christians who live both in the here-and-now and the there-and-then are to make the reign of God present by means of their active love of God and neighbor, but such manifestations will vary according to circumstances. Individual Christians will make different decisions about how best to do it. In fact, the moral dimension of the kingdom is so difficult that it is only begun in evangelism and will continue to develop as the new Christian matures.

In the years since *The Logic of Evangelism* was first published, many of the issues which prompted its creation have changed. Evangelism courses are now part of the standard curriculum for seminaries, and a great many popular and academic books on evangelism have been produced. Many of these books were directly influenced by *The Logic of Evangelism* and include citations from it. For example, Abraham's two successors in the McCreless Evangelism Chair at Perkins have incorporated the concept of the kingdom into their own definitions of evangelism.[14] Within a wider Wesleyan scope, a number of collective volumes on evangelism, some written by former students and colleagues, have emulated Abraham in their serious theological approach to the subject. These works explore scriptural, patristic, and Wesleyan understandings and practices of evangelism, presenting divergent views, but exemplifying similar concerns about academic rigor. Significant among them are *Considering the Great Commission: Evangelism and Mission in the Wesleyan Spirit*, edited by Stephen Gunter and Elaine Robinson, *Transforming Evangelism: The Wesleyan Way of Sharing Faith*, edited by Henry Knight and F. Douglas Powe, *The Study of Evangelism: Exploring a Missional Practice of the Church*, edited by Paul Chilcote and Laceye Warner, and *World Mission in the Wesleyan Spirit*, edited by Darrell Whiteman and Gerald Anderson. Many others have made solo scholarly contributions to the study of evangelism, including Walter Klaiber's *Call and Response: Biblical Foundations for a Theology of Evangelism*, Robert Tuttle's *The Story of Evangelism*, and Bryan Stone's *Evangelism After Christendom*.[15]

The specific dimensions of evangelism covered in chapter six of *The Logic of Evangelism* have also been the subject of further discussion. Conversion has been the subject of a number of books written out of the Wesleyan tradition. Noteworthy among them is *Conversion in the Wesleyan Tradition*,

14. Heath, *Mystic Way of Evangelism*, 13; Jones, *Evangelistic Love*, 23.

15. See Gunter and Robinson, *Considering the Great Commission*; Knight and Powe, *Transforming Evangelism*; Chilcote and Warner, *Study of Evangelism*; Whiteman and Anderson, *World Mission in the Wesleyan Spirit*; Klaiber, *Call and Response*; Tuttle, *Story of Evangelism*; Stone, *Evangelism after Christendom*.

edited by Kenneth Collins and John Tyson, which includes a broad sampling of scholarly reflection on different aspects of conversion. Conversion from a variety of religious positions was examined in *Handbook of Religious Conversion*, edited by Newton Malony and Samuel Southard. Jason Vickers, a former student of Abraham, also published a chapter in which he expanded Abraham's thesis that the separation of conversion from the sacraments results in a seriously limited theology. On a more general level, scholars have become much more open to the discussion of conversion and a number of specific studies have appeared. Examples include Dong Young Kim's *Understanding Religious Conversion: The Case of Saint Augustine* and Bruce Hindmarsh's *The Evangelical Conversion Narrative: Spiritual Autobiography in Early Modern England*. A retrievalist impulse, which began in nineteenth-century Catholic theology and has provided the basis for the RCIA, is now thriving within Protestantism as well, supplementing the work on conversion with massive information from patristic sources. An important example of this work is Thomas Finn's *From Death to Rebirth: Ritual and Conversion in Antiquity*.[16]

Since 1989, baptism has also been the subject of considerable academic attention. Thomas Finn's *Early Christian Baptism and the Catechumenate* and Everett Ferguson's *Baptism in the Early Church* provide the student of Baptism with a wealth of historical information about how baptism was practiced and understood in the early Church. Swedish scholar Lars Hartman has contributed *"Into the Name of the Lord Jesus": Baptism in the Early Church*. Abraham's former student Paul Gavrilyuk has added his own history of baptism and the catechumenate with *Histoire du Catéchuménat dans Léglise Ancienne*. More widely, British scholar Juliette Day has written a number of historical studies on the baptismal literature of the fourth and fifth centuries, including *Baptism in Early Byzantine Palestine 325–451* and *The Baptismal Liturgy of Jerusalem*. In addition, Robin Jensen has researched ancient baptism-related architecture and art, providing the scholarly world an additional perspective on this subject.[17] British evangelicals

16. Collins and Tyson, *Conversion in the Wesleyan Tradition*; Malony and Southard, *Handbook of Religious Conversion*; Vickers, "To Know and Love God Truly"; Young, *Understanding Religious Conversion*; Hindmarsh, *Spiritual Autobiography*; Finn, *From Death to Rebirth*.

17. Finn, *Early Christian Baptism*; Ferguson, *Baptism in the Early Church*; Hartman, *"Into the Name of the Lord Jesus"*; Gavriljuk, *Histoire du Catéchuménat*; Day, *Baptism in Early Byzantine Palestine*; Day, *Baptismal Liturgy of Jerusalem*; Jensen, *Baptismal Imagery in Early Christianity*; Jensen, *Living Water*.

have also produced collective volumes on baptism, including *Baptism, the New Testament and the Church: Historical and Contemporary Studies in Honour of R. E. O. White* and *Dimensions of Baptism: Biblical and Theological Studies*. Included in the first of these volumes is a discussion of baptism as "inaugurated eschatology" by Neville Clark,[18] echoing Abraham's understanding. A Wesleyan approach to adult catechesis and baptism has been offered by Daniel T. Benedict.[19]

Finally, as Abraham predicted, while there is presumably a general agreement that the great commandment is central to any understanding of Christianity, there is no consensus on how the great commandment is to be fulfilled. This is especially true for the second provision. The very substantial literature dealing with this topic falls into several categories. The various manifestations of liberation theology concerned with loving the oppressed make up a large percentage of this work. In addition to the often-discussed issues of political, economic, and gender-related oppression, this category has recently come to include acts of religious intolerance, especially against Muslims.[20] A second category, which is currently much more prominent than it was in 1989, deals with issues regarding human sexuality. Yet another focus of moral thought is concerned with loving one's non-human neighbors, the natural world, and its occupants.[21] Thoughtful Wesleyan contributions in this area include *Holiness as a Root of Morality: Essays on Wesleyan Ethics: Essays in Honor of Lane A. Scott*, edited by John S. Park, and *The New Testament and Ethics: A Book-by-Book Survey*, edited by Joel B. Green.[22]

---

18. Porter and Cross, *Baptism, the New Testament and the Church*; Porter and Cross, *Dimensions of Baptism*; see also, Clark, "Initiation and Eschatology," 337–349.

19. Benedict, *Come to the Waters*; Hindman and Benedict, "Come to the Waters."

20. Nazila, *Challenge of Religious Discrimination*; Nussbaum, *New Religious Intolerance*; Haney, *Great Commandment*.

21. Tigert and Tirabassi, *Transgendering Faith*; Cupit, *Ethics in the Last Days*.

22. Park, *Holiness as a Root of Morality*; Green, *New Testament and Ethics*.

Chapter Seven

Catechesis and the Spiritual Gifts

Paul L. Gavrilyuk

My copy of The *Logic of Evangelism* was a gift from its author, with a dedication dated January 1994. William Abraham and I had met only a few months earlier, beginning what would turn out to be one of the closest and most enduring friendships of my life. At the time, Abraham was already a prominent church leader, a renowned theologian, and a highly respected seminary professor with a large following of graduate and postgraduate students at the Perkins School of Theology. I was just a disoriented international student, newly arrived to the United States from the post-Soviet world, who came to Perkins in order to pursue a master's degree and then continued with a doctorate under Abraham's supervision. As a mentor, Billy Abraham was extraordinarily generous with his time, despite his very demanding schedule of research, teaching, and speaking engagements. I found myself learning as much from him in the classroom as I did when we played table tennis or shared a meal together. As a philosopher, he allowed a tremendous amount of intellectual freedom to his pupils, and it was this freedom that made the gravitational pull of his thought irresistible. As a result, he has shaped not only what I think of various theological subjects, including evangelism and initiation, but also, and more importantly, how I approach them in practice.

The Logic of Evangelism has provided a major inspiration for my reflection upon and engagement in catechetical work. On a theoretical level, the book offered a captivating account of evangelism as a practice of initiation into the kingdom of God, patterned upon the catechetical practices of the early church. The book, as well as the conversations with its author, provided a major impulse for my own research on the patristic catechumenate with a view to recovering its rich resources for today's church.[1] At the heart of the patristic catechumenate, as it came to be developed towards the fourth century AD, was the practice of the transmission, explanation, and recitation of the creed during baptism. The period of the forty days leading to the celebration of Easter was usually dedicated to regular catechetical instructions, which for such early church leaders as bishop Cyril of Jerusalem and Bishop Theodore of Mopsuestia, consisted in a detailed commentary on the articles of the local baptismal creeds. Alluding to this practice in *The Logic of Evangelism*, Abraham identifies the Nicene Creed as the doctrinal core of Christian initiation. He defends his choice both against the biblical minimalists, who would reduce the creed to a summary of the good news based in scripture, and against the confessional maximalists, who would prefer to use the Articles of Religion (or their equivalent) instead of the creed. According to *The Logic of Evangelism*, the process of initiation and passing on of the Christian message required three irreducible and interdependent elements: scripture, creed, and episcopate. Abraham writes:

> To separate out the Scriptures as isolated and superior to the creed is arbitrary; both represent decisions of the church that were inspired by the Holy Spirit to safeguard the community's heritage and identity across time and in the turmoil of history. This in turn required institutional oversight or episcopacy, for there is no point in having a canon and a creed if there is no social mechanism or institution to ensure that they are kept at the heart of the life of the community.[2]

In this passage from the seventh chapter of *The Logic of Evangelism*, one begins to discern the emerging contours of the concept of the "canonical heritage," which Abraham will introduce a decade later in his magnum opus, *Canon and Criterion in Christian Theology*.[3] In addition to the scripture, creed, and episcopate, a fully developed understanding of the "canonical heritage" will come to include the canons of liturgy, sacraments, iconography, church architecture, and saints. In Abraham's later articulation:

---

1. Taking a break from my dissertation research at SMU, I wrote *History of the Catechumenate in the Early Church*, which was published in Russia in 2001 and subsequently translated into French and published by Éditions du Cerf in 2007.

2. Abraham, *Logic of Evangelism*, 149.

3. Abraham, *Canon and Criterion*.

The church possesses not just a canon of books in its Bible but also a canon of doctrine, a canon of saints, a canon of church fathers, a canon of theologians, a canon of liturgy, a canon of bishops, a canon of councils, a canon of ecclesial regulations, a canon of icons, and the like. In short, the church possesses a canonical heritage of persons, practices, and materials. . . . The canonical heritage of the church functions first and foremost soteriologically. It operates as a complex means of grace that restores the image of God in human beings and brings them into communion with God and with each other in the church. Each component is primarily an instrument to be used in spiritual direction and formation.[4]

As an Orthodox theologian, I found much in this proposal that was very congenial during my years at Perkins. As the years went by, I came to appreciate more and more that Abraham's category of the canonical heritage was no mere restatement of the contested relationship between scripture and tradition. Instead, the concept of the canonical heritage provided an effective toolkit for identifying and articulating the interconnections of the different elements that helped to safeguard and transmit the faith of the church through the centuries. Like the pieces in a Chinese box, the components of the canonical heritage interlock with each other, comprising a coherent structure. The main function of the canonical heritage was to provide abundant means for initiating believers into the life with God and providing ample sustenance to their faith.

On a practical level, *The Logic of Evangelism* was a call to resourcing and reviving early Christian initiatory practices in contemporary missionary and catechetical work. Since this was an area in which I had no experience, I took Abraham up on his offer to follow him on his missionary journeys to the nascent Christian communities in countries as distant as the former Soviet republic of Kazakhstan and Costa Rica. Both churches were planted by the Methodist missionaries from the United States. Over time, both communities developed indigenous leadership, which continued to be mentored and supported by the North American missionaries.

The communities in Karaganda, Kazakhstan, consisted largely of ethnic Russians and Germans, with some Kazakhs, in the midst of a majority Muslim population, all scarred by decades of the repressive Soviet regime. These communities were very fragile because of the outside pressures and the absence of episcopate. What their young leaders lacked in pastoral

---

4. See Abraham, "Canonical Theism." This volume was a "Perkins project" because the contributors were Abraham's former doctoral students and Perkins faculty.

experience, theological education, and institutional support was compensated by the freshness, vibrancy, and sincerity of their faith, as well as by their charismatic zeal. For me, it was a bit like a descent into the chaos of the early church, with fresh debates over old doctrinal issues (such as free will vs. predestination, the use of icons, and so on), a reinvention of the canon of the sacraments (I distinctly recall an altar call at a Sunday service that felt like an improvised sacrament of confession), and an emerging episcopal oversight (accompanied by a tacit agreement not to call it so officially). Perhaps, most importantly, the Karaganda communities abounded in the gifts of the Spirit, manifesting themselves in prayer meetings (at which I witnessed various leaders uttering long *ex tempore* prayers, reminding me of the "prophets" described in the early Christian text, *Didache*), but also infusing this loosely organized whole with the patterns of worship and even leadership structures. In the young churches planted in Kazakhstan, I did not observe the more familiar dynamic of the Spirit testing the boundaries or challenging the institutional structures because those structures were so thin on the ground. On the contrary, to my great surprise, I witnessed the Spirit as a creative force behind birthing some elements of the canonical heritage of the church, in particular, its liturgy, sacraments (especially confession), episcopate, and the core biblical doctrine. There were, of course, some notable omissions. For example, the group's biblicism precluded the deployment of the creed as anything other than a summary of scripture. In addition, iconography was suspect on the grounds that it verged on idolatry, especially as practiced by the local Orthodox, who returned the favor by treating these young Protestant communities as sectarian. Yet, sectarian or not, the fruits of the Spirit were on display among these freshly catechized Christians: they showed considerable concern for the most vulnerable among them, were not afraid to confront the social problems in their community, including various addictions and chemical dependency, and actively worked towards providing the church members with better education and better employment opportunities. In these circumstances, our missionary teaching, which I expected to be a somewhat arid academic exercise, has offered numerous unforeseen possibilities to connect the "cognitive side of initiation," as *The Logic of Evangelism* calls instruction in the fundamentals of faith, with the "spiritual disciplines." In addition to an intense teaching routine, Abraham was called upon to preach, serve, and offer pastoral counseling. I had a unique opportunity to learn by immersion the things that no book about missionary work could possibly teach me.

Ten years later, in 2010, Abraham took me on his missionary trip to an Evangelical Methodist Seminary in Costa Rica. Our target audience consisted primarily of Methodist pastors, who shepherded their communities in a predominantly Roman Catholic country. We were offering an equivalent of intense "continuing education" courses to people, many of whom had graduated from the seminary years ago and had considerable pastoral experience. Since Costa Rican Christianity, in general (and our group of pastors in particular), was influenced by the charismatic movement, some conversations naturally brought us to the topic of the spiritual gifts and sanctification. Within this topic, of special import was a discussion of the gifts of healing with a particular concern about the abuses associated with the prosperity gospel, which had made considerable inroads in Central and Latin America. If I remember correctly, the prosperity gospel inspired little sympathy and much protest, whereas the attitudes towards its nemesis, liberation theology, were more conflicted. Since my growing up amidst the crumbling Soviet system did not instill in me any profound trust in the economic or moral soundness of Marxist principles, I preferred to keep my lecture firmly within the historical boundaries of patristics.

This, in turn, dictated that I deal with another controversial topic, that of deification. My announcement of the classical exchange formula, "God became human so that humans could become gods,"[5] elicited numerous puzzled, even scandalized looks among my Costa Rican students. The scandal was not much alleviated by my attempt to qualify Athanasius's bold statement by pointing out that the persons of the Trinity are divine by nature, whereas humans could only become the children of God by adoption or participate in the life of God by grace. I was told of a local church leader who claimed to be divine and had a financially flourishing healing ministry on the internet. In truth, I was completely unprepared to deal with the challenge at hand and, with some exasperation, retreated into a Wesleyan safety zone by making the following assertion: "What your tradition calls 'entire sanctification,' the patristic tradition calls 'deification.'" I realized, of course, that the concepts of "sanctification" and "deification," whatever their overlap, were, strictly speaking, not synonymous. Still, I was relieved that the danger of a serious misunderstanding had been averted, for to assert deification was to side with a local charlatan, who imagined himself a deity. Whatever one might think of my attempt to salvage my theological reputation, the crucial Christological reference and, more importantly, a

5. Athanasius, *On the Incarnation*, 54.

connection between the divine incarnation and the healing of the human nature, had been "lost in translation" from one cultural context (that of late antiquity) to another (that of contemporary Central America). What was gained in this context was a sense that the doctrine of sanctification was not primarily about the theological distinctions between the work of the second and the third persons of the Trinity, no matter how important those distinctions were, but was, first and foremost, about Christian life deeply touched by the abiding presence of the Holy Spirit. I was profoundly moved by the fact that at the end of our lecture cycle, our students laid their hands on both of us and collectively prayed for God's healing power in our lives. In Costa Rica, as in Kazakhstan, there was a deep connection between theological education and spiritual formation, in Abraham's terms, between a "university-level catechesis" and spiritual disciplines.

The connection between the theoretical and experiential dimensions of Christian formation is something that my own Orthodox tradition finds deeply congenial. From the Byzantine ascetic writings, enshrined in the *Philokalia*, to such contemporary classics as Vladimir Lossky's *Mystical Theology of the Eastern Church*,[6] one finds in the Christian East a powerful impulse towards an integration of the life of the mind with the matters of the heart. This impulse also finds its expression in Charles Wesley's poetic call to unite "knowledge and vital piety," which in turn was inspired by the pietistic reading of ancient Christian sources. In the initiatory practices of the early church, the catechumenate had both didactic and ascetic dimensions. The didactic dimension consisted of hearing the Christian proclamation, reading the scriptures, and receiving the foundations of the faith as enshrined in the creed. The ascetic dimension consisted of fasting, prayer, vigils, exorcisms, and penitential practices. The purpose of such practices was the purification of the heart with the purpose of disposing oneself to the reception of the Word of God and the activity of the Holy Spirit. The operating assumption was that the cleansing of the soul was required for the proper apprehension of the Christian teaching.

Baptism developed as a rite marking a decisive break with the practices of the pagan past, as a point of renunciation of the powers of the demonic in one's life, and as incorporation into the body of Christ. The anointing with chrism (sanctified oil) in the sacrament of chrismation (or confirmation) was a mark of the baptizand's belonging to Christ and a seal of the gift of the Holy Spirit. The baptismal Eucharist had the features of the messianic

---

6. Lossky, *Mystical Theology*. French original in 1944, first English translation in 1957.

banquet, which made possible the believer's taste of the kingdom of heaven. The Eucharist is an invitation to "taste and see that the Lord is good" (Ps 34:8); in other words, the ritual offers an opportunity to spiritually perceive the goodness and mercy of God. To put this differently, Christian initiation is more than education when it is combined with the ascetic "cleansing of the doors of the senses," it offers a framework for cultivating spiritual perception.

While spiritual perception—the discernment of the presence of God by the "eyes of faith" or the "ears of the heart"—may take different forms, one particular example comes to mind. In the early 2000s, I briefly joined a group of Orthodox Christians who were engaged in ministry at a medium security prison in Lino Lakes, Minnesota. We would travel to Lino Lakes with a local choir, a few icons, incense, and sanctified (non-sacramental) oil. We could not serve the Eucharist, as most of the inmates were not Orthodox, and the Orthodox Church does not practice "open communion." We would begin our services by pointing to our "visual aids," the icons of Christ and the Theotokos, and briefly explaining our core beliefs. While the icons inspired some curiosity, our audience was not particularly taken with either our expositions of doctrine or my sermons. What captivated the inmates was music, incense and, most of all, the (non-sacramental) anointing that was offered to all who desired at the end of the service. The anointing consisted in signing the foreheads of the inmates with the sign of the cross by means of a cotton swab dipped in sanctified oil. The ritual is quite similar to the (sacramental) anointing of the sick practiced on the Holy Wednesday of the Passion Week (the week before Easter). It was clear to me that the anointing we performed at Lino Lakes made a deep and lasting impression on the inmates and was possibly their favorite part of the service. The cross, as a sign of victory over sin and death, was a tangible sign of divine protection. It seemed that neither the words of the sermon nor even the words of scripture moved them as strongly as being "branded" with the sign of the cross on their foreheads as a sign of belonging to Christ. The experience was both physical and more than physical. One felt that, through some tangible means, God's intangible presence and guidance were powerfully communicated. It would be impossible to judge whether this anointing, repeated only twice a year, had a lasting impact on the prisoners' lives. It is clear, however, that when combined with the "cognitive side of initiation," such as the reading and interpretation of scripture and the exposition of the fundamentals of faith, the anointing could become an integral part of the reconciling work of the Holy Spirit and could serve as a vehicle of healing. In this respect, one was reminded of the gospel story of the woman with the issue of blood, who received a healing touch of God simply because she dared to touch Jesus, without going through a catechetical program.

Nevertheless, a functioning and sustainable catechetical program is a crucial instrument of initiation. Since Orthodox communities in the United States are often modest in size and have a small number of catechumens in any given year, it generally makes sense for different Orthodox jurisdictions—the Orthodox Church in America, the Greek Orthodox Archdiocese, the Antiochian Orthodox Archdiocese, and others—to unite their catechetical efforts. In my area, the local pastors offer what we call a Cooperative Catechism of the Minnesota Eastern Orthodox Christian Clergy Association (MEOCCA). The course consists of fourteen two-hour sessions, offered once a week in the evening, to accommodate the busy schedules of working adults. The course is loosely based on the articles of the creed and includes the following themes: God—Holy Trinity; creation, humankind, fall, and messiah; Incarnation, Theotokos, and the saints; Christ's work and teaching; Church's birth, mission, and structure; Councils, creeds, Bible, and tradition; Sacraments: baptism, chrismation, confession, unction, Eucharist, prayer, marriage, and monasticism; the last things and living Christian life; and Orthodoxy in America. This particular topical structure has endured without any major modifications for the past fifteen years. The course is taught by about ten local clergymen from different jurisdictions, which allows the inquirers to get a feel for the different "flavors" of Orthodoxy found in the Twin Cities. The target audience is quite mixed, from non-Christians to future spouses of Orthodox Christians, to those who have been firmly planted in other Christian communions for many years and have an interest in the Eastern tradition but no strong desire to join the Orthodox Church. Some have been exposed to very rigid and legalistic forms of the Orthodox ethos; others struggle to integrate their prior experience in other Christian communions with what they receive in their catechetical classes. Some are attracted by the doctrinal riches of Orthodoxy; others are curious about smells, bells, and icons; still others are interested in mining the resources of the ascetical tradition as alternative forms of spirituality.[7] Upon completing the course, all are invited—through baptism for the unbaptized and through chrismation for most others—to join local congregations.

7. Slagle, *Eastern Church in the Spiritual Marketplace.*

Some take a small dip and move away; others drift through Orthodoxy towards yet another expression of faith; others hesitate to join the Orthodox Church because of the culture shock to friends and relatives; still others, in a few years, find their feet firmly planted in the Orthodox tradition. On the one hand, some converts among intellectuals surprise me in that their reason for joining was non-cognitive, such as the beauty of the liturgy; on the other hand, the converts less inclined to the life of the mind on occasion confess that they were brought to the church by reading a particular book. The visitors that step into the Orthodox place of worship for the first time usually find themselves surrounded by icons and are drawn into the story of salvation through images and music. While the stories of conversion differ considerably, both the cognitive and non-cognitive factors play an equally formative role in the process of initiation into the church.

In the field of mission and evangelism, the leadership of the Orthodox Church has much to learn from other Christians. I owe my primary schooling in this arena to the prolific scholarship and captivating personal example of Billy Abraham. For me, he communicated the spirit of those venerable Oxford divines who were ever ready to exchange their splendid scholarly attire for the humble robes of an itinerant preacher and missionary. It is this spirit that I, as an Orthodox Christian, received as one of the most precious gifts of the Holy Spirit. Over the years, this spirit has quietly shaped and sustained my own work, as it has also nourished our friendship.

Chapter Eight

The Logic of the Creed in Evangelism

ELIZABETH MOREAU

Introduction

SEVERAL YEARS AGO, WHILE I was teaching a class on the Nicene Creed, a participant objected to my claim that the Nicene Creed was the unifying force in Christianity. The woman legitimately could be considered a superior biblical scholar; she reads both ancient Greek and Hebrew and was a long-time participant in Bible Study Fellowship[1] before becoming a teacher in the study. Her counter-claim was that the Bible is the source of Christian belief, and Christians are unified by the grace of Jesus Christ.

I mention this anecdote because I believe her view to be the most widely accepted opinion—and largely unquestioned assumption—about the source of Christian faith in Protestantism today. In fact, since Martin Luther nailed the ninety-five theses on the Wittenburg Door in 1517, the prevailing understanding among the people who became known as Protestants has been that the source of all knowledge about God, creation, human beings, our salvation, and the like—in essence, the source of knowledge about Christianity—is Scripture. But is this true?

Acknowledging the contentious debates of the Early Church, especially in and around the being and nature of Jesus Christ, the Christian Church

---

1. Now an interdenominational study located in San Antonio, Texas, Bible Study Fellowship originated in a home study begun by Audrey Wetherell Johnson in the mid-1950s. British by birth, Johnson was a missionary to China who settled in the Baptist denomination in Southern California following her retirement from the mission field.

was largely united for approximately a thousand years, as in, there was a single church that encompassed the whole of the Christian Body without regard to race, nationality, language, or politics. Central to the identity of Christians individually and the Church corporately as it spread throughout the ancient world was the Creed formulated at the Council of Nicaea (AD 325) and finalized at the Council of Constantinople (AD 381). In response to the outbreak of what was likely a form of Arianism in Spain in the late sixth century, the *Filioque Clause*[2] first appeared in the Western Church. The vehement response from the Eastern patriarchs[3] regarding change to the universally accepted Creed from the fourth century initially prevailed in the West, but over time, the clause continued to reappear in Western Christianity until it became normative among most Western Christians. While Pope Leo seems to have embraced the double-procession of the Spirit in ninth-century Western Christianity, he was unwilling to alter the Creed officially, largely because of his commitment to church tradition and unity. However, under his leadership, the Roman Church ceased to use the Creed at all. Early in the eleventh century, the *Filioque Clause* was added to the Nicene Creed in the West per the request of the German Emperor, Henry II, an act that ultimately led to the Great Schism of 1054 between the Eastern and Western branches of the Christian church.[4] Thus, one can reasonably claim that the church was united for a thousand years, at which time, as a result of a change in the Creed, it became two churches. The church remained two distinct bodies for another five hundred years.

The midst of celebratory fervor surrounding the birth of Protestant-ism five hundred years ago may not be an optimal time to call attention to the unintended consequences of the Reformers' renewed emphasis on the primacy of the scripture in the face of ecclesial abuses. Or, perhaps, the flurry of theological and ecclesial reflection offers exactly the best occasion to evaluate the fruit of the Reformation, particularly as this topic relates to William J. Abraham's *The Logic of Evangelism*. Separation from the an-cient churches, East and West, began with Martin Luther, but reform and division also had significant support from Huldrych Zwingli, John Calvin's

2. *Filioque* is Latin for "and the Son" and refers to the procession of the Holy Spirit.

3. Change to the Creed was anathematized at the Third Ecumenical Council in Ephe-sus in AD 431.

4. To be sure, the Great Schism occurred in response to other complicating factors in addition to the clause, a full account of which is beyond the scope of this work. The relevant point for our purposes is that the root theological cause of the division was a change to the Nicene Creed.

theological predecessor in the Reformation. Ultimately, Luther and Zwingli, as well as Calvin, remained theologically at odds, which gave rise to the Lutheran and Presbyterian denominations, respectively. In the centuries following the Reformation, the rallying cry of *sola scriptura* resounded across the West, and Christianity fractured into an estimated—and astonishing—thirty-four-thousand denominations,[5] of which more than fifteen hundred exist in the United States, all claiming "biblical authority." Casting further suspicion on the Protestant confidence in *sola scriptura*, merely fifty years after the Reformation—using the Bible alone—anti-Trinitarians in Poland wrote the basis of the Racovian Catechism[6] that became the foundational document of the Unitarian Church. Put succinctly, the Christian church existed as one church for a thousand years, as two churches for five hundred years, and disintegrated into thirty-four-thousand churches over the subsequent five hundred years with the advent of the Reformation and the doctrine of "scripture alone," the Western church. The first division of the Church, resulting in two churches—East and West—occurred with the alteration of the Church's universal Creed. The second division within Christianity occurred when the Creed was set aside entirely, at least in the sense of its primary role in defining the content of Christian faith, resulting in the perpetual fragmentation of the church. The only logical conclusion to be reached is that "scripture alone" is not sufficient for purveying the substance of authentic and life-saving Christian belief. Moreover, in no sense might we reasonably claim that the Bible unifies Christians.

The Need for the Nicene Creed in Christian Initiation and Formation

Since the publication of *The Logic of Evangelism* thirty years ago, the old, mainline denominations have divided over interpretations of scripture, each side claiming it has the correct understanding, even as membership in the denominations continues to decline in greater percentage than Christian belief in the West is declining. Currently, the United Methodist

---

5. This number probably appears somewhat exaggerated in that the number includes individual churches unaffiliated with any denomination. However, a fair count of denominations and movements over the last five centuries would not be less than twenty thousand, still a shockingly high number when one considers only one Bible is being used.

6. First published in 1602.

Church—my own denomination—is in the throes of contentious division regarding the interpretation of scripture in the presenting issue of homosexuality, as was the case in recent divisions among other historically-mainline Protestant denominations. Both sides claim authentic Christian belief and discipleship and appear to be at an impasse in their conclusions. While the ecclesial hierarchy calls for "holy conversation," leading to unity in Jesus Christ, most cognizant persons are clear there is no feasible solution to the theological conflict. In addition, most United Methodist clergy on both sides of the argument are essentially aware that two entirely different systems of belief are in play. The irony of the consistent appeals to scripture as the authority in the face of implacable disagreement reveals the unrealistic naiveté of our hope for unity based on scripture alone.

In a recent live-stream event intended to show the ease and feasibility of "holy conversation," two members of the clergy, one on each side of the divide, sat together and cordially explained and defended their differences by appealing to the Bible. On the one side, a hermeneutic of Jesus' love for all and Paul's dismissal of human distinctions[7] was the basis of interpretation. Such a basis is hard to argue in that Christians today define virtually all interaction with each other and with the world around us through the lens of the love of Christ and the value of all people, regardless of being and circumstance. On the other side, a "scripture interpreting scripture" sort of hermeneutic appeared to apply, likely a modified form of biblical inerrancy, taking into consideration the full biblical witness. As before, this hermeneutic is difficult to dismiss given the emphasis on the validity of the whole of scripture, as opposed to select teachings.[8] The extremely civilized and congenial conversation certainly provided the space and time for what could only be described as a friendly and gracious discussion, but the most obvious point was never mentioned, much less made clear: for all the professional camaraderie of the conversation, there was no resolution. In fact, there was not even a movement toward resolution because both members of the clergy were deeply committed to their interpretations of biblical Christian teaching, and neither learned anything new from each other, at least nothing that would persuade either party to a change of view. In short, while the conversation may have been an excellent example of

7. "There is neither Jew nor Gentile, neither slave nor free, nor is there male and female, for you are all one in Christ Jesus" (NIV, Gal 3:28).

8. Worth noting, both hermeneutics used in the discussion were selected as decisions of human reason, each participant applying the hermeneutic he considered most reasonable and appropriate.

how to treat one another with respect and good manners in the discussion of theological differences, that example is the only thing accomplished. No minds were changed. No unity was developed. No resolution to the conflict became apparent, something I suspect both pastors knew before the conversation ever began.[9]

What has all of this to do with the discussion of the ancient Creed included in *The Logic of Evangelism?* The central thesis Abraham puts forward is that evangelism rightly considered is best construed as initiation into the kingdom of God.[10] The book includes a review of other, more typical and familiar forms of evangelism, such as proclamation, church growth, and witness, but argues for a fresh perspective that reflects the spread of Christianity in the Early Church. Christianity was born in historical events that were revealed in God's supernatural involvement and activity in history, specifically, the inauguration of the reign of God on earth. The evangelistic spread of Christian faith through the earliest converts and their successors was the outcome of their experience of and participation in the dawn of God's rule.

Long before Christianity was a legal religion in the Roman Empire, long before there was an ecumenical council, and long before there was a canon of scripture, the framework for what became the universal Creed could be found throughout the earliest churches, a framework grounded in the historical activity of God. That framework is what Abraham refers to as the *rule of faith*,[11] and it was the intellectual basis upon which membership in the church depended. The rule of faith was critical for evangelism in the first century because becoming a Christian required a complete transformation of one's intellectual commitments. The rule of faith inevitably developed for those coming out of the world and into the church because they were moving from a world ruled by a plethora of Greco-Roman gods and goddesses and into a world where the Triune God of the Christians reigned. Moreover, the rule of faith was nothing more and nothing less than belief in the concrete actions God took in the world and for the world, as well as the logical conclusion of those actions. "Do you believe that God the

---

9. Given that the UMC has debated this issue for forty-four years, the participants in the holy conversation very likely could have knowledgeably articulated the other's position. The problem is not that church leaders and pastors do not understand those with whom they disagree. The problem is *that* they disagree. No amount of conversation will change that fact.

10. Abraham, *Logic of Evangelism*, 13.

11. Abraham, *Logic of Evangelism*, 145–52.

Father is the Maker of all things?" as opposed to the primordial gods and goddesses of Earth, Love, the Underworld and Darkness; "Do you believe that Jesus Christ is the Son of God, who was born to a virgin, died on a cross, and rose from the dead for the salvation of the world?" in contrast to the host of demigods that move through the world doing good or harm as they will; "Do you believe in the remission of sins?" over and against the prevailing need to appease the numerous gods with sacrifices and gifts. These are first and foremost intellectual decisions, requiring individuals to decide which system of belief was credible to them—because changing one's beliefs about the origin and nature of all existence alters the whole of one's life and living, priorities, morality, behavior, attitudes, and more. The invitation to join the church was predicated upon this change of one's entire belief system and intellectual assent to the truth of the claims about God's actions in history. Paul's admonishment to "be transformed by the renewing of your mind" (Rom 12:2) takes on enormous significance when the extent of the conversion of the intellect is considered seriously. For all the changes wrought in an individual who came to faith in Jesus Christ—in worship, prayer, religious experience, and moral formation—the intellectual criterion for becoming a Christian was the rule of faith, the precursor of the Nicene Creed.

As Christianity declines in the United States, the cognitive dimension of conversion echoes the same complexity and dramatic change required of the intellect. Precisely because Christian faith and belief have become less and less distinctive in Western culture, the church would be wise to explore again the depth and breadth of the content of faith outlined in the Nicene Creed, both for those curious about joining the church and, sadly, probably for the majority already within the church as well. To be a Christian is to maintain certain intellectual commitments that shape every aspect of human life, from birth to death and every step in between. Every human being holds some form of integrated cognitive structure, recognized or not, through which he or she makes sense of life and the world. For Christians, that structure is defined in the Nicene Creed. The failure of the church to invite the mind of Christians and converts into the exploration of God's astounding actions in God the Son and through God the Spirit is tragic indeed. The church engages in tacit rebellion against God when it does not take responsibility for the transformation of the mind and, if Paul is correct, the likelihood of renewal is greatly diminished.

Objections and Responses Today

Objections to the use of the Nicene Creed in a central role in the life of the church today abound. The first objection comes from those denominations committed to the bible alone that refuse to introduce anything beyond what is written in those sixty-six books.[12] The good news is that they take the scriptures seriously. The bad news is that such a church will be perennially confined to the religious sentiments of those from whom the church or denomination originated. Few means of reconciliation between opposing points of view exist and, therefore, disagreement over readings of scripture leads to schism. Though it sounds familiar, this scenario is not the predominant dilemma faced in the United Methodist Church or other old mainline denominations. The circumstances surrounding conflict and division actually are more complex.

In a recent social media conversation among United Methodist clergy, a discussion arose about the Nicene Creed. Going into the 2016 General Conference of the UMC, a petition was submitted to add the Nicene Creed to the official doctrinal standards of the denomination. The petition did not pass the Committee on Faith and Order and never reached the floor of General Conference for a vote. So it was that several Methodist clergypersons were discussing why the subject was introduced and why anyone would think adding the Nicene Creed would be a good idea. The most telling part of the discussion was the assumption that the Nicene Creed held no value to the United Methodist Church or even Christianity today. Several comments indicated a near-complete lack of familiarity with the Creed, compounded by the certainty of its irrelevance in modern times. The only positive comment came in the form of its beauty and usefulness in worship if one understood the Creed as metaphorical language.[13] One cannot help but wonder what clause of the Creed is best understood metaphorically. Was creation by the Father a metaphorical event? The death and/or Resurrection of the Son, perhaps? The forgiveness of sins? How one could

---

12. Abraham addresses this objection more thoroughly on page 145.

13. Theories of the metaphorical nature of religious language are derived from the deconstructionist school of philosophy proposed by the French philosopher Jacques Derrida (1930–2004). Briefly summarized, deconstructionism allows meaning to be assigned to texts and language by the reader—not the author of the text itself. In this way, virtually anything said or written can be reinterpreted to the intellectual preferences of the recipient of the material. In essence, written text has no meaning in itself until such time as the reader assigns meaning to it.

gain any rational or even aesthetic meaning from a metaphorical Creed is unclear. Moreover, the likelihood that early Christians were prepared to deny everything they once knew at the risk of death for metaphorical beliefs is far-fetched at best. Were the martyrs merely metaphorically dead? Were tongues cut out and hands cut off only in a metaphorical sense? The spread of Christianity in the first, second, third, and even fourth centuries cannot be explained by metaphorical convictions, which leads to the greater and more difficult challenge to the Nicene Creed in contemporary Protestantism.

Academia today widely dismisses significant portions of the New Testament and early church writings as untenable because the societies from which they arose were not advanced societies. Vast stores of knowledge available to us were not available then. Notably, if the religious and theological academy believes this to be true, then necessarily those training to be clergy are learning this perspective as well. Yet, for all the sophistication of much contemporary theological study, such a view is simply implausible. To argue, for example, that miraculous healings were not supernatural at all, merely the natural course of events occurring among a people who knew nothing of germs, is an obfuscating investment of mental energy. One does not need to know anything about germs and disease to know a person was sick and is now not. Knowledge of the inner workings of the body's brain and nervous system is not required to recognize an individual who could not walk is now walking, nor is expertise in ocular physiology needed to know a person who was blind now is not.

In another example, a parallel argument speaks to the intellectual insupportability of the Resurrection of Jesus Christ. Science has now shown, with the cessation of oxygen at death, brain cells immediately begin to die and brain deterioration starts, thus rendering physical resurrection impossible. Hence, only the uneducated and superstitious could believe in the Resurrection. Christ's Resurrection is also challenged by the absence of resurrections elsewhere in history. While such theological proposals are generally rigorous and thorough, the assumptions driving the need for such arguments seem to be void of basic common sense. Leaving aside the obvious point that the Creator of all that exists would not be stymied by human death, the single, most fundamental claim of Christian faith and belief is that in Jesus Christ the fullness of God was present in the Second Person of the Trinity, and the Son came into the world for the salvation of the world through the forgiveness of sins and through the defeat of death.

It follows that, if God has saved the world and initiated his rule in history toward His desired conclusion, a repeat performance would be unnecessary. Furthermore, the idea that people in the ancient world were simply too gullible to realize there was no Resurrection is, again, an impressive expression of intellectual prowess untethered from common sense. One need know nothing about the processes that take place following death to know people do not rise afterward. The first century population knew what dead was, and they likewise knew death was final. Had there been other resurrections during their time, that certainly would take some of the polish off the shine of Jesus' Resurrection, rendering it passé and of little import. Yet, history completely defies the suggestion that the birth, life, death, and Resurrection of Jesus Christ were metaphorical, physically impossible, or insignificant. To the contrary, Christian faith and belief have survived and spread in every century, every culture, every language, and every political system for the last two thousand years.

The last major objection to the Creed addressed here is the claim that the Creed makes specific claims to truth and, therefore, the use of the Creed is a form of exclusion, shutting out those who disagree[14] and, in the process, creating strife and division. But when history is reviewed, as above, it is clear the Creed actually has the opposite effect. The *absence* of the Creed as the normative framework for Christian intellectual formation results in endless division, not the presence of unity. Division is coming yet again; it is inevitable. When compared to the traditional beliefs of the Christian Church, the sophisticated theologies of twenty-first century Western religious academia move intellectual commitments so far as to be incompatible with traditional Christian intellectual convictions. No means of resolving disputes between opposing perspectives exists. Unity of belief about the meaning of Christian faith is unattainable and, therefore, ultimately, there can be no unity in the body or in worship.

---

14. I hazard to ask the question, but why would anyone want to be "in" something with which they disagree? No amount of invitation and openness could convince me to join the Ku Klux Klan (nor the Hindu or Islam religions, nor many other bodies of belief in the world today), but I hardly feel excluded because I am not a part. There is no reason even to desire to be a part, and thus, whatever exclusion exists is totally irrelevant. Moreover, the church would be well advised to learn the distinction between inclusive invitation and inclusive content.

Restoring the Nicene Creed Today

Abraham's review of evangelism in its current forms details the limitations of each school of thought, but what he offers in that regard is simply the intellectual framework for understanding the decline of Christianity in America. Effectiveness is a self-evident failure in the face of the numbers. While the United States population has increased by nearly 30 percent since 1990, the latest polls show Christianity in the nation has declined by about 14 percent over those years. In unhappy comparison, during the same period, the United Methodist Church dropped precipitously by over 35 percent. Clearly, however we construe evangelism, efforts have failed. As church leaders scramble to find ways to halt decline and search for attractive forms of ministry in an ever-increasing environment of skepticism and, sometimes, hostility, Abraham's vision of evangelism as inauguration into the Kingdom of God offers a clear and provocative alternative. The way forward is not one that Protestants have typically tried, but instead embraces the fullness of the Gospel that propelled Christian life and faith in obscure places among groups of people around the world following two millennia.

The United Methodist Church has much to commend in its doctrinal standards, Articles of Religion, ecclesial structure, and more. However, as evidenced by the contentious and irreconcilable internal debates, the UMC has also failed to shape the Christian mind with the depths of the intellectual heritage passed down through the centuries. Lost in speculative systems of thought, Methodism becomes less relevant as it goes to great lengths to find ways to be more. The saving Gospel of Jesus Christ is not relevant for any human being—until it is. Modifying, reinterpreting, or outright changing the substance and meaning of Christian faith not only does not make Christianity somehow more relevant but rather serves to diminish the Christian life. Western culture is drenched in secularism and materialism, with a subtle but pervasive ethos of meaninglessness and hopelessness. The fields are indeed ripe unto harvest, but one wonders if the United Methodist Church in its current iteration has the necessary tools for harvesting, much less threshing. As Abraham rightly points out, construing evangelism as initiation into God's kingdom involves a variety of disciplines, not the least of which is the formation of the mind. The contemporary church needs to reclaim the faith defined in the Nicene Creed, for the Creed alone is the unifying force in all of Christianity, the articulation of the acts of God in history into which human beings may join, culminating in the final and eternal reign of God. In the search for answers and guidance, Protestants in general, and Methodists in particular, ignore the insight offered by Abraham in *The Logic of Evangelism* at their own peril. The events of history that revealed the advent of the reign of God remain the decisive core at the heart of Christian faith and life. Those actions taken by God, however far removed in time from today, are no less life altering and no less important for the whole of the world now than they were when they occurred. In Christianity, a resurrection is always coming. If we would experience resurrection in Protestantism, we first must be initiated into the kingdom of God where resurrection occurs.

Chapter Nine

The Wider Ecumenism

Robert J. Hunt

I read William J. Abraham's *The Logic of Evangelism* for the first time in 2006, when it was the required textbook of a course I was asked to teach at the last minute. My previous twenty years of teaching had been outside of the United States. In these contexts, Christians were a disempowered—if not absolutely threatened—minority. They were struggling to understand and engage with a multi-religious society that included their own, non-Christian family members.

Perhaps because I was coming from those contexts, the conclusions Abraham drew through his approach to the wider ecumenism seemed commonsensical (and, I thought, readily acceptable by almost all of my former students)—that evangelism is the effort to win people to the Christian faith.[1] Relatively unaffected by the challenges of modernity that Abraham discusses, my students regarded this effort as a founding principle of the church. After all, most were themselves converts from non-Christian communities. Therefore, in considering what Abraham calls the "wider ecumenism," I would also suggest that we take seriously the experience of converts to Christianity. This, in turn, will demand that we take seriously the communities from which they have come as communities with their own integrity as well.

I make this point because I knew from my experience outside the American cultural context that modernity is not the "universal" in which all Christians are learning what it means to follow Christ. I also knew that

1. Abraham, *Logic of Evangelism*, 212.

Christians found a fully coherent (if complex) world of discourse in the Bible, out of which the world could be fruitfully comprehended, and engaged with the basic truths about God and humanity revealed in Christ.

This understanding of the Bible seems to me a central thesis of Abraham's entire book. His statement: "The claim that Jesus is the only way to salvation is analytic" relates to his earlier assertion that "the fundamental, determining factors in our thinking about evangelism do not rest on the analysis of the modern world but on the internal logic of the Christian gospel."[2] This insight releases the Christian from the endless and largely hopeless task of continually revising the claims of the Bible into the ever-shifting logics of contemporary worlds of discourse. It allows Christians to focus on contextualization, making the logic of the gospel comprehensible in the widely different cultures out of which contemporary ways of life emerge.

Moreover, this approach releases the task of contextualization from the absurdity of claiming that knowledge of a historical figure, unknown to most humans for all of human history, is somehow the only means by which any human may have a relationship with God.[3] In the context of the post-Christian, historically-conscious West, such a claim merely seems irrational. In the context of emerging churches of converts in a multi-religious society, however, it becomes the deeply offensive claim that good, decent persons, as one's own grandparents, are doomed to hell because they were born in the wrong place and at the wrong time.

It is not too much to say, then, that the greatest problem for evangelism in much of the non-Christian world is two-fold. One problem is how certain Western evangelists and their minions believe they are exalting God by forcing a decision, condemning to hell the ancestors and friends of potential converts; a second is their doppelgänger contemporaries, who avoid this problem by teaching that conversion was never really necessary, thereby denigrating the experience of heroic converts to Christ.

If we understand, however, that the claim of the Bible is that *Christ* is the only way to the Father—rather than the witness of a particular evangelist in a particular time—we can also make a claim that is both credible and humane. If we insist that some choice for or against faithful entry into God's reign is nonetheless necessary, we may also equally make a claim

2. Abraham, *Logic of Evangelism*, 204, 217

3. Abraham, *Logic of Evangelism*, 213

consonant with human reason and experience across all societies and religious cultures.

The Problem of Pluralism

These considerations set the stage for Abraham's chapter on "The Wider Ecumenism." As he points out, the contemporary debate over evangelism in relation to a world of non-Christian religions is not primarily about how to do evangelism but rather whether evangelism is a legitimate expression of Christian faith at all. It is a debate over the nature of the religious world and particularly over the world religions.

For Abraham the core of this challenge is what he calls the "revisionist impulse" with regard to revelation. Instead of understanding revelation as something that breaks into human life, revisionists understand revelation as something that emerges as individuals and societies recognize a text or person as significant: a sign or indicator of the nature of reality as they have experienced it.[4] The application of this revisionism in the domain of religion (or of a world of religions) results in *pluralism*, or the theological assertion that there are multiple paths to the same God. It is this pluralism that Abraham challenges and corrects in his chapter on the wider ecumenism.

Therefore, I would suggest that if we are to understand the church's evangelistic task in the twenty-first century more fully, we must realize that pluralism is not founded in just the revisionist impulse regarding revelation associated with the rise of modern liberal theology. Indeed, necessary for a pluralistic theology of religions is the assumption that *religion* is a fundamental category of human social and psychological behavior and that there exist many religions, each of which we may construe as possessing an account of human faith.

This idea was initially challenged by Wilfred Cantwell Smith in *The Meaning and End of Religion*, whose critique of the term religion continues to inform the field of religious studies even if he was regarded as a pluralist.[5] Since the publication of Abraham's book, the pluralist assumption has been shown to be untenable from two additional perspectives. The first has come from theologians of religion such as Schubert Ogden and Mark Heim, who have demonstrated with some care, albeit using different approaches,

4. Abraham, *Logic of Evangelism*, 214

5. Smith, *Meaning and End of Religion*.

that different religions do not understand themselves as having the same purpose and end.[6] Put simply, the assumption that different religions represent different paths to life in God's reign imposes on the so-called religions a Christian framework for analysis that is not valid in the case of the phenomena under observation.

A second critique of pluralism, coming from within the academic study of religion, is equally important. In her seminal work, *The Invention of World's Religions: Or How European Universalism was Preserved in the Language of Pluralism*, Tomoko Masuzawa demonstrates how the very concept of distinct world religions, which provides the basis on which Abraham conceptualizes "the wider ecumenism," reinforces Smith's observation that the language of pluralism derives from a discourse that emerges with modernity in the West, rather than a dialogue among people of different cultures about how humans across a variety of cultures actually represent themselves to themselves and others.[7] Tomoko shows that pluralism is not simply a contemporary theological framework constructed by European Christians to make sense of the plurality of cultures encountered in early modernity.[8] Following Smith, she shows how pluralism is also the consequence of extending the idea of religion as a description of *Christian* behavior to become a category of *human* behavior within Western universalism; it allows the West to both comprehend and colonize otherwise unique modes of being human with an essentially self-referential discourse.

If this is the case, and I believe that Masuzawa's work is compelling, then any form of pluralism is misleading—including those forms of Christian theological pluralism that *reject* the many paths, one God hypothesis. A pluralism that understands the so-called world religions as *rivals* with one another (and with Christianity) is also a product of Western universalism. When this plurality makes the realm of religion one of competition, where each religion pits its exclusive, universal claims against the others, it affects the Christian attitude toward non-Christian religions. Paganism and heresy can be supplemented or corrected with the truth. But rival claims to truth can only be rejected and replaced. The result is what is commonly called "exclusivism."

---

6. Ogden, *Is There Only One True Religion*; Heim, *Salvations*.

7. Masuzawa, *Invention of World Religions*.

8. The task described by Langton Gilkey in Hick and Knitter, *Myth of Christian Uniqueness*, 37–50.

Or, and this was the genius of the 1910 Missionary Conference in Edinburgh, the so-called world religions can be comprehended within Western universalism as precursor religions to Christianity, as was implicit more than a century earlier in Schleiermacher's taxonomy of religions in *The Christian Faith*, "The Diversities of Religious Communions in General: Propositions borrowed from the Philosophy of Religion."[9] Instead of replaceable rivals, we can view religions as ways in which God prepares people to hear the good news, just as we can appreciate other cultures and civilizations as important steps on the path toward fulfillment by European civilization. The result is commonly called "inclusivism."

Thus, exclusivist and inclusivist understandings of Christianity in a world of religions must be considered alongside the form of pluralism that Abraham addresses directly. There is not one pluralist impulse in Western Christianity, there are three. And although regarding other religions as either rivals or precursors to Christianity doesn't directly undermine the evangelistic mandate that is Abraham's major concern, it does distort that mandate in ways that will affect the calling of persons into God's reign. Making the contemporary concept of "religion" more problematic for evangelism is that it is not part of the thought worlds of those entities identified as religions, a problem identified by Smith.[10] This observation is almost self-evidently true in Buddhism, Hinduism, Judaism, and other so-called primal religions, yet it is also true of Islam, which recognizes these and other "religions" (*din* in Arabic) as the products of distinctive revelations, something these so-called "religions" do not claim about themselves.

In other words, the problems that Abraham identifies with pluralist theology and the challenges faced by evangelists are created not merely by the subjectivism of modern Christian theology but by the very conceptual framework within which "the wider ecumenism" is understood. This argument, in turn, suggests that rather than developing a robust "theology of religions" as Abraham suggests, what the church may need to do is reject the category of religion as a description of the wider ecumenism altogether and turn to more biblical and classically Christian ways of identifying the varieties of human society, personhood, and experience instead; the different "households" that make up the human family.

If this argument is true, then the Christian theologian seeking to understand evangelism in a global context faces two challenges. The first is to

9. Schleiermacher, *Christian Faith*.

10. Smith, *Meaning and End of Religion*, 43

seek an understanding of the culturally diverse human world built on more realistic and more Christian foundations than that of philosophies, sociologies, anthropologies, and psychologies of religion. The second is to explore how the Bible illuminates the contemporary experience of being human within this wider ecumenism and how that bears on the task of evangelism.

The Human in Culture in Biblical Context

To answer the first of these challenges, we must find a more authentically Christian basis for conceptualizing the human world in which the church proclaims the gospel. A starting point for a Christian theology of the wider human world is surely the Bible, which continually acknowledges the existence of the entire human family in all its diversity, but in ways that precede and do not depend on contemporary forms of discourse around religion.

It is helpful to recognize at the outset, then, that neither the language of the Bible nor that of pre-modern Christianity has any concept of "religion" consonant with the modern usage of the term. There is no Hebrew equivalent of the word "religion" and contemporary conceptualizations are unknown in the Hebrew Bible. In some translations, such as the NIV, the English word does not even appear in the Old Testament. The Greek term θρησκεία, which, in most English language New Testaments, is translated "religion," is limited to ritual behavior and possibly an attitude of worship. It does not approach the full-bodied definition of a culture system offered by Geertz and typical of contemporary usage.[11] Indeed, the limits of its meaning are indicated by the fact that Luther translated it "Gottesdienst" and modern German translations translate it "Frömmigkeit." Neither translation makes use of the German "Religion."

Rather than being concerned with religion as a culture system, the Bible is concerned with certain, specific aspects of what we call religion, such as: belief in gods or God; ethical behavior based on God's covenant with humankind (and specifically God's covenant with Israel); the struggle of humans with those powers that cause alienation, hunger, poverty, and disease, manifestations of God's power and grace in the world; and finally, the ways in which human affiliation draws people closer or further from God's reign. Many, but not all, aspects of religion in the contemporary sense are present in the Bible, but are never put together as culture systems.

---

11. Geertz, *Interpretation of Cultures.*

This essay will not attempt to explore how these biblical categories relate to the modern concept of religion, but some examples may be suggestive of the project before us.

We might begin, therefore, with the challenge faced in applying the biblical prohibition against the worship of multiple gods to evangelism among people whose cultural practices include what appear to be multiple deities represented by idols: for example, the peoples of the subcontinent and East Asia. This allows the recognition that an invitation to enter into God's reign does not begin with a call to change religions but rather for individuals to examine their relationship with their objects of worship in light of Christ's kingdom.

The Christian critique of idolatry is that it substitutes the creature for the creator. In the case of Hinduism and Buddhism, however, the apparent idol is not understood as a creature; in Hinduism, the creator remains the ultimate object of worship, while Buddhism deconstructs the concept of a Creator entirely. To say, "You cannot enter God's realm worshipping idols," returns the rejoinder from that Hindu or Buddhist that "these objects are in fact the doorways into God's reign. They are no different from your icons, except they are rooted in the culture and history of South Asia rather than the culture and history of the Middle East."

This is not, however, an impasse. For the evangelist knows that the real conversation here is not about idolatry, something that would have been as laughable to educated Greeks in Paul's time as it was to Paul. It is about the ways in which human sin distorts those windows into mirrors and, ultimately, self-worship, a conversation that resonates with both Buddhist and Hindu traditions.

It is why we cannot reduce an invitation into God's reign to a condemnation of false religion and idolatry or even an invitation to exchange one set of icons for another. Instead, it is an invitation to appraise whether a person's practices (or religion, in the narrow New Testament sense) draw one closer to or deflect one away from a relationship with God. It is really a conversation about how Jesus Christ is as different in kind from the avatars and bodhisattvas as pictures and statures are from God.

We can see this move in 1 Corinthians 8–10, which provides an example of how such a conversation plays out for those initiated into God's reign. The apostle Paul offers a substantial and subtle critique of both idolatry and the complex ways in which even those who no longer worship idols per se are drawn into its effects through "food offered to idols." Paul's analysis exposes the folly of idolatry and the way in which it can become a point of contact with the demonic. Then, going further, he addresses the complex considerations that those who have been freed in Christ from both folly and the demonic must nonetheless make as they care for their Christian brothers and sisters. Paul takes into account the personal, transcendent, and communal aspects of God's reign.

In a context in which self-identified Hindus and Buddhists focus their attention primarily on philosophy—or the correct correlation between the mind and reality—a somewhat different evangelistic conversation might take place. Again, it would not begin by rejecting affiliation and practice (neither of which is accurately represented by the names applied to these so-called religions in any case). Rather, it would examine the resonances between historical attempts in South Asian philosophy to account for transcendent reality and Christian teaching. Timothy Tennent's essay, "Trinity and Saccindananda in the Writings of Brahmabandhav Upadhyaya," is one example of entering into this kind of philosophical conversation with the gospel.[12]

Tennent's essay is in the tradition of Paul's short speech to the Athenians as reported in Acts 17. Luke reports that Paul distresses over the large number of idols in Athens. Yet he chooses to engage these Athenians from the philosophical perspective of how God (defined in a way that they will recognize) makes Godself known. Paul praises the Athenians for being very "religious" (or "devout," depending on the translation, a different root in Greek than the word translated "religion" in James). If he is being ironic, then it is an irony that these philosophers will easily recognize as coming from within their own traditions. Again, Paul does not address these Athenians as members of a *religion* but rather as philosophers and practitioners within specific cults, whose reflections and practice need redirection if they are to enter into God's reign.

A witness intended to initiate entry into God's kingdom might also focus on engaging non-Christians in ethical concerns, both narrower and wider, while recognizing that establishing such a dialogue depends on disentangling it from discourse about sin. It is almost a truism to say that people of different cultures share certain values and ethical mandates based on those values. Indeed, this is something that Christians should expect, given that scripture teaches that all humans share in a common covenant

---

12. See Brockman and Habito, *Gospel among Religions*, 182–93.

with God first given to Noah. On this basis, Christians are able to stay engaged, even across cultures, in the broader social context of their witness.

Here, we might look at Paul's argument in Romans 2:14–16, or later, in Romans 12:17, where Paul refers to "what is noble in the sight of all." Throughout Romans, as elsewhere, Paul understands that Christian behavior will appeal to a universal sense of what is good and appropriate. Even the ruling authorities should be obeyed out of conscience, even though they are not Christian (Rom 12:5). Paul understands that the followers of Jesus are embedded in human societies within which those outside of their community are also due respect and honor. In their moral behavior, Christians participate in a wider social discourse over what is right and wrong. Religion in the modern sense, then, plays no role here, even though some among both the Greeks and Romans might well appeal to their gods as a source of moral authority.

What the invitation into God's rule requires, therefore, is not contentiousness over moral values but rather pointing out the grip that sin has on human life and accepting by faith that Christ forgives and overcomes sin. The problem of ethnical discourse with the Gentiles is not so much that they are bad as that they are *foolish*, unaware of the larger context in which they seek to act ethically. It is why *evangelistic* discourse over ethics is not necessarily about the difference between right and wrong; the question posed by God's reign is the difference between what all humans know is right and our inability to do what is right (Rom 7:16). The answer to that question, God's grace revealed in Jesus Christ, is what overcomes a foolish self-reliance.

While the witness of scripture is clear regarding the grip of sin on human life, it does not reduce the human condition as to ignore the reality that human beings struggle with other unseen forces. These forces—e.g., demons, disease, hunger, poverty, and others—provide both points of contact and opportunities for witness.

In my years in Asia, the problem of demon possession and exorcism arose on a regular basis. All of the major ethnic and self-identified religious groups in Malaysia recognized demon possession as a problem; all of them had exorcists of one kind or another. In that situation, the witness to the gospel was not merely that the power of Christ overcame the power of demons in a person's life; it was that entering into Christ's reign forever freed a person from the power of demons. Christian exorcism was not a change of allegiance or exchange of power among the invisible forces of the world.

It was the freedom to choose one's allegiances free of coercive power. Jesus warned his followers about the dangers of not filling the empty place left when God casts out unclean spirits (Luke 11:24-26). Yet he does not demand of those so freed that they follow him as much as they exercise their freedom to proclaim their experience of God's reign (Luke 8:38).

This freedom can be the beginning of an initiation into a community dedicated to preserving and extending this experience of freedom, not only from demons but from disease, hunger, and poverty as well. In Romans 12–15, there is an extended essay on how the freedom of a Christian from the "principalities and powers" must always be tempered and shaped by the mission of freeing other members of the community from those same powers. Christian witness in Paul's letters recognizes that joining the body of Christ gives believers a new community in which they experience freedom from the oppressiveness of the old. And the freedom found in Christ grants the possibility of continuing those relationships while respecting those who have not yet cultivated the freedom to move freely between the Christian community and that of their past.

This complex freedom sets the reign of God apart from the exclusive demands of other human communities. To use the concept articulated by Jesus in John 14, the Christian can be both in and not of the world. Therefore, becoming a Christian is not simply about choosing one community rather than another, except to the extent that one must live out both the freedom and responsibility of allegiance to Christ alone. The nucleus of a Christian community in any one place might be a biological family, yet the *household* was much larger, extended by the fictive kinship of all those who were children of God. They were communities rooted in Jewish ideas of families called by God but (at least initially) stripped of ethnicity and geography and grounded only in the ongoing experience of God's reign through common worship. For decades, Jews in these Christian families could continue to participate in the Jewish community until a crisis internal to Judaism led to their expulsion. From the Christian perspective, there was no conflict in this dual affiliation.

When conflicts arose later in Christian history, however, it was because the Christian allegiance to Christ made it impossible for Christians to participate in the cult of earthly rivals to Christ. As noted above, there was no conflict with the *governing authorities* as such. The conflict arose from the divinizing of Rome and the Caesars and the demand to worship at their altar. Later Christian exclusivism would arise only when Christianity became the official cult of Rome and of the emperor's family. Christians viewed pagan worship as a sign of divided political loyalties and even treason. Beyond the boundaries of that political dispute, the problem of dual affiliation is one of continual discernment as to what is at stake in terms of loyalty to Christ. That this is not always obvious to informed and reasoned observers can help explain the centuries long "rites controversy" in relation to Chinese ancestor practices.[13]

In the contemporary "wider ecumenism," then, it is critical to see that choosing to follow Christ is not a change of "religion," but rather a decision to be initiated into Christ's rule. This involves affiliation with a new community of Christians who provide the social location and fellowship for continued growth in Christ. Whether it requires a change in other affiliations and practices will often be an open question, a question requiring considerable spiritual discernment. When Naaman returned to his home country, for example, having acknowledged, "There is no God in all the world except the God of Israel," Elisha sent him in peace, even though he confessed that at times he would be required to bow down in the temple of an idol (2 Kings 5).

The long arc of the biblical narrative is shaped by the conflicts that arise because Israel and—later—the Christian community are constantly called into the liminal space between the people of God and those to whom they are obliged to witness. In Matthew 10:34, Jesus quotes Micah, "Do not think that I have come to bring peace to the earth; I have not come to bring peace, but a sword" (Mic 7:6). In both the original context of this quotation and in Jesus' preaching, "bringing a sword" is not a call to create conflict; it is telling the signs of the times when the inevitable conflict between God's kingdom and the claims of other powers breaks into even the most basic of human affiliations: the family.

Unfortunately, when we misplace these verses into the imaginary conflict between "religions," we create conflict that is far from being a sign of God's reign. We realize that there is more to the picture, for if these verses serve as they should serve, as reminders that the powers of this world (in many forms) will push back against the claims of God's reign on the followers of Christ, they become part of the spiritual discernment necessary to navigate the multiple affiliations of the modern person. Evangelistic analysis, therefore, should revolve around questions of allegiance to human

13. Brockman and Habito, *Gospel among Religions*, 73–80.

social structures only to the extent that those allegiances specifically hinder entry into God's reign. Paul's advice regarding food offered to idols in 1 Corinthians 8–10, then, becomes practical here. For Paul, the problem of idolatry is not of the idols per se, but of the potential for new believers to fall back into the folly of idolatry through the apparent affirmation of earlier systems of affiliation. Most notably, the specific problem is the liminal space occupied by believers who still participate in family and other social gatherings around food.

This experience of liminality corresponds to my own experience living in Singapore and Malaysia. For those Singaporeans and Malaysians who had never been associated with a community dedicated to idol worship, visiting a temple was of almost no spiritual consequence. Nor did they have any particular personal problem eating food placed quite literally on altars before symbolic representations of spiritual forces. It was a different matter for those still affiliated (primarily through family) with the temple, temple worship, and dinners at which food offered to deities was regularly present. Then the temple and the products associated with it continued to pose the spiritual danger of drawing them back into the old world of fear from which Christ had freed them. Their fellow Christians had to respect the nascent struggle for freedom if there was to be a full witness to the breaking in of God's reign.

At the same time, indirect participation in temple worship is not the primary matter that is a danger to Christians related to affiliation. For the apostle Paul, *participation* is a much wider concern, and it includes all forms of behavior not consonant with participation in the life of the risen Christ (1 Cor 6:15–16; 2 Cor 6:14; 1 Tim 5:22). The contemporary evangelist moves in and out of a wide variety of cultural realms, including those created by post-modernity. He or she must be concerned with many forms of affiliation that, while not obviously religious, are nonetheless detrimental to living in fellowship with those being initiated into God's reign.

The Human in Culture in Contemporary Discourse

Having indicated the problems with *religion* as a category for theological reflection and having suggested other approaches for evangelists engaged with the wider ecumenism, it is important to turn to another aspect of the wider ecumenism. Here, a "plurality of cultures and societies" has emerged as the essential environment in which contemporary persons seek to understand themselves and what it means to be human. In this context, the revisionist impulse identified by Abraham not only leads to religious pluralism, the revisionist impulse also leads to an understanding of the wider world as a world of resources and challenges to those seeking human meaning and authenticity. We may understand the human person as a seeker after meaning, whose quest he or she defines not only by the goal but also by the richness of the resources accumulated in order to reach that goal. That richness of resources we may in turn understand as allowing human meaning and authenticity to take place within what Charles Taylor calls *the immanent frame*, the frame that explicitly denies the eschatological dimension of God's reign so critical for Abraham's understanding of the Gospel and thus evangelism.[14]

In this situation, the evangelist faces not so much the problem of religious pluralism undermining the necessity of evangelism, as persons engaged with a hyper-plurality of possibilities for constructing a meaningful life. These possibilities emerge from either the plurality of ways of seeking meaning that accumulate in almost all cosmopolitan cultures, or what Charles Taylor calls a "super-nova" of ways of finding meaning within the immanent frame.

The fractured culture of the nova, which was originally that of elites only, becomes generalized to whole societies. This reaches its culmination in the latter half of the twentieth century. And along with this, and integral to it, there arises in Western societies a generalized culture of "authenticity," or expressive individualism, in which people are encouraged to find their own way, discover their own fulfillment, "do their own thing." The ethic of authenticity originates in the Romantic period, but it has utterly penetrated popular culture only in recent decades, in the time since the Second World War, if not even closer to the present.[15]

While the conditions of secularity that Taylor describes may be unique to the West and its colonial outposts, the *nova* effect that he describes is not so limited culturally. There have existed since the "axial age" cities whose cosmopolitan nature makes available multiple resources for constructing a personal orientation within a variety of imagined transcendent environments. Paul met something like this in Athens.

It was also found in the medieval Muslim world of the Abbasid dynasty, where a rich ferment of Greek philosophy mingled with Islamic

14. Abraham, *Logic of Evangelism*, 27–32
15. Taylor, *Secular Age*, 299.

revelation and the Asian philosophies taught by Buddhists and Brahmins that traveled along the Silk Road. An urban civilization grew up in which affiliations of spiritual seekers crossed the lines demarcating the Jewish, Muslim, Christian, and Zoroastrian communities. At least for some social classes, aesthetic expressions and meditative practices rather than ritual practice and community affiliation became the dominant modes for seeking a relationship with the transcendent.[16]

Something like the nova of choices and its ethic of authenticity was also present in Xian, Delhi, and other Asian cities even earlier as waves of trade, conquest, and migration brought new possibilities for imagining the human relationship with the transcendent. In those cities, persons combined the recognition of a vast multiplicity of unseen powers with long-standing philosophical traditions that moderns would label "humanistic." In Buddhism, Taoism, and the Brahminic tradition, for example, knowledge of the world (including the unseen world) begins and ultimately ends with the human as knower of the world in all its dimensions, rather than the one who is known by God and depends on a revelation to know the self.

The result is the centrality of the devotee and whatever source of authentic relationship with transcendence is most personally appealing. It is common in Southeast Asia to find both Chinese and Indian temples with shrines dedicated to Jesus. Here, Christ is sometimes informally included in the pantheon of deities because of his association with mission schools and the valued experience of education but equally because of the attractiveness of his teaching and miraculous power found in the four Gospels.

More formally, the modern Vedanta movement of Ramakrishna and the Red Swastika Society among overseas Chinese represent sectarian communities built on the appropriation of multiple religious resources, including not only traditional Asian teachers but Muhammad and Jesus as well. Ramakrishna, founder of Vedanta, is reported by his followers to have fully entered into each of the world's religious traditions in succession over a period of several months, learning and appropriating from each what would become their central values.

We often characterize this old/new world as one of *faith* rather than religion, with the word *faith* indicating a ubiquitous human quest for meaning that takes many specific forms. This, in turn, opens up the possibility of not only a plurality of communities whose members share the same faith, but of persons with "multiple religious belongings" whose *personal* faith

16. Hodgson and Spotswood, *Venture of Islam*, 221.

is equally an *idiosyncratic* faith. Their world is one in which there are not merely many paths to the same God but rather multiple alternatives to God as the environment (transcendent, immanent, or both) in which we find meaning.

Within civilizational approaches relating to the transcendent commonly called religions, we are able to capture some of these perspectives; others are imagined or re-appropriated to the more ancient resources: the so-called "New Age." What was common several decades ago in Southeast Asia in culturally-complex, cosmopolitan environments, a home or local shrine with a pantheon of deities from various religious traditions is increasingly common in the homes of Westerners who still maintain membership in Christian communities.

In this environment, we can see the greater ecumenism, rather than as a world of communities with which a person might affiliate and between which dialogue is necessary to establish a shared social space, as a vast trove of possible sources and approaches to constructing a meaningful life. Christianity is not one of many religions but is both a collection of resources for constructing personal faith (regardless of one's communal affiliations) and a potential center around which other resources may be gathered.

There arises for the evangelists, then, the subtle problem already present in many Christian communities, that the gospel of the reign of God has been reduced to one of many possibilities for finding human meaning. Jesus is less a ruler and more in terms of a guru, a "life coach," or even as a "lifestyle concierge."[17] The reign of God is a vision of human flourishing realized by willing hearts within what Taylor calls the "immanent frame," or a variety of mythical renditions of the transcendent end of humanity. Either way, people will not so much be initiated *into* God's reign as they will *appropriate* some idea of the reign of God into their own personal quests for meaning. They will conceive of the world both as a place where many paths lead onward and outward to the same God as well as a place where all paths potentially lead inward and downward to the fully realized self.

This insight has become a common basis of "interfaith" or "interfaith dialogue." Communities and their leaders, as well as some divinity schools, now identify themselves as "interfaith" in the sense of bringing a variety of spiritual resources to bear on the task of constructing human meaning.[18] In this context, the term "spiritual" indicates not so much a connection

17. Lehman, "Joel Olsteen Worships Himself."

18. World Awake, "Interfaith Seminaries."

with that which lies beyond the immanent frame, the Spirit of God, as it indicates that part of human personhood that engages in the search to find meaning and the sources of meaning the seeker finds.

In keeping with the cultural tendency to remain within the immanent frame, it is the *cosmic* rather than *transcendent* environment for human seeking that often comes to the fore, keeping the quest grounded in immanence, even if of immense proportions.[19] Science can thus become both a form of this quest and a resource for those along the way. In *The Presence of the Infinite: The Spiritual Experience of Beauty, Truth, & Goodness*, Steve McIntosh offers one of many examples of bringing together science with a variety of religious teachings seeking to show the unitary (and immanent) nature of reality and the variety of ways humans can legitimately experience and place themselves within it.[20]

In this inter-*faith* environment, evangelism, as Abraham understands it, must undertake a dual task. First, it must place *both* the sources of meaning found in Taylor's "supernova" *and* the search for meaning/identity/ authenticity that characterizes contemporary personhood in the appropriate theological context. Second, it must understand and facilitate the crisis of meaning, *the conversion that turns individual quests for meaning from a process of acquisition to one of surrender.*

A World of Witnesses

An initial approach to a biblical understanding of Taylor's supernova of possible sources of meaning is to recognize that the Bible sees the world of nature, culture, and society (the immanent frame) as the realm in which God's reveals God's plan for humanity: "Go and tell John what you see and hear" (Matt 11:2–6). The world is the realm of signs or witnesses to God's presence and activity. In a sense, if one is looking for the meaning of human authenticity, then the "world" is the place to look.

However, there is an important difference between *witnesses* to God, as either *resources* in the human quest or as *windows* into the divine. While the modern quest for meaning gathers resources and looks for those "thin" places where transcendence is more immediately felt, the witness draws the human gaze away from itself and its purposes and then toward God's reign.

19. Taylor, *Secular Age*, 507.

20. McIntosh, *Presence of the Infinite*.

Resources and windows are passive, to be consumed or approached on the quest for meaning. Witnesses are active, diverting seekers and pointing them toward the ultimate source, context, and end of human personhood. When the psalmist looks to the hills, it is not because the hills inspire, but because they bear witness to a living God (Psalm 151). As the prophet reminds us, God acts and endures: "Lift up your eyes to the heavens, and look at the earth beneath; for the heavens will vanish like smoke, the earth will wear out like a garment, and those who live on it will die like gnats; but my salvation will be forever, and my deliverance will never be ended" (Isa 51:6).

When we look at the biblical description of a world of witnesses, several things of consequence emerge. The first is that we must take into account the workings of God's Spirit in the world: the Spirit's presence and call transforms passive resources into active witnesses; God's Spirit speaks the language of the human spirit and addresses the human. When the Spirit of God falls on the prophet, history begins to disclose and draw people toward God's reign. In the Psalms, God's Spirit is the guide, leading in the ways of God. In Exodus, the Spirit leads the people to give their resources, providing them then with the skills necessary to create the Ark, whose visible presence will draw them toward God (Exod 31:3; 35:21). More directly, in Job, God is the one who confronts Job with the majesty of creation in a way that points Job beyond himself to God. We can see this as well with Jonah where Nineveh is in the domain of God's concern, calling people to repentance as a sign pointing to God. Paul also emphasizes this in worship: "When we cry, 'Abba! Father!' it is that very Spirit bearing witness with our spirit that we are children of God" (Rom 8:15–16).

When Gerald Manley Hopkins writes, "the world is charged with the grandeur of God," the word *charged* is no mere metaphor.[21] It is only because the world is charged with God's grandeur that God's glory can be seen by human eyes in the world. This is in contrast with even the romantic understandings of nature as an inspiration or their equivalence in the recognition among scientists of nature as the realm of wonder. A world absent of God's Spirit allows at best a mere inkling of feeling that occurs when the human spirit comes upon the precipitate of God's rule, whether in nature or culture. Therefore, the theological question concerning a world of resources is whether any apparent source of meaning is actually a possible habitation for God's Spirit and the witness of God's Spirit through it. If not,

21. Hopkins, "God's Grandeur," 27.

then whatever other virtues were a resource, it cannot be a witness and thus cannot draw seekers out of themselves toward God's reign.

The Seeker for Meaning

When we look at the supposed resources for meaning from a biblical perspective, we begin to see how a contemporary person on a quest for meaning is different from the pilgrims in the Bible. Pilgrims in the Bible have both a destination and a guide, whether the pilgrim is Abraham, Israel, or the Christian community. It is a journey punctuated by witnesses, whether in inanimate, animate, human, or spiritual form. The journey is emphatically not the goal; even if the journey itself is rich with meaning, it is not meaning*ful* without reference to its end.

From a biblical perspective, the pilgrim is on a quest in which sin and, therefore, redemption are essential features. The world is not only a world of witnesses but also of temptations and false witnesses. It is not that the vast riches of the world are not capable of deeply enriching each human life. The problem is the human tendency to grasp them and turn them inward, to *consume* these creatures of God rather than to *listen* to the witness of the Spirit through them, drawn out into the vastly greater world of transcendence that they represent. The manna that fed the Hebrews is a case in point. As a daily link to their God's providence, it is good. Accumulated for mere consumption, it rots.

For the pilgrim, then, human sin is the desire to use those "thin" places that are doorways into unseen transcendence as a voyeur who stands and stares and takes in everything there is to see but never steps through for fear of losing the self. It is the human tendency to follow every guide and to find authenticity in what we create, rather than in the one who creates us and who assures us—that *we* end up becoming the meaning of the quest rather than the One who directs us to witness. Jacob's dream of a ladder at Bethel is not the end of a quest for a vision but the beginning of a commitment to make the LORD his God and press on in the task set before him (Gen 28:10–22). Bethel is a place Jacob must leave behind.

I have used Taylor's term "supernova" rather loosely to indicate the available resources from which we can seek meaning and out of which we can create it. Properly speaking, what Taylor speaks of is the supernova of possibilities for constructing human identity. It is the possibilities within this supernova that we must critique from a biblical perspective, for in the

Bible, not every experience prepares pilgrims for their end and not every path guides them toward it. For this reason, not every journey is worthwhile. Some journeys, as noted above, may be absent of God's animating Spirit. Others, as Taylor identifies, are beyond a human capacity to shape toward fulfillment. The answer in the Bible to this predicament, this form of "cross-pressuring," is God, who alone who can release us from the human bondage to sin and redeem the human experience of turning inward, redirecting us into the ways of the reign of God.

This insight is what Taylor communicates in his chapter on "conversions."[22] We cannot accumulate what we desire apart from transcendence. Transcendence can occur only when the world, in its manifold dimensions, becomes a living witness to God's reign, drawing us out of our immanent frames.

Conversions

How can such a change, a conversion, happen in a world that offers such a variety of possible sources and approaches to meaning and authenticity that a person's life may end before it becomes obvious that the journey was not enough? In the Bible, such conversions occur when divine intervention in the human story meets the human capacity to be reoriented toward God's realm; they occur when God's self-disclosure meets human faith. God as the seeker finds the human.

What is noteworthy as we approach conversion in the wider ecumenism, therefore, is that in the Bible, we discover how we not only narrate conversions but also how there is an essentially narrative quality to them; both humans and societies are understood to have their identity in terms of their story, primarily their story of engagement with God. Change is *enacted*, whether by God or by God's people.[23] Given that we live in an age moving away from essentialist understandings of identity toward narrated identities, this divine action appears the key to evangelism in the midst of the human quest for meaning. As Calvin Schrag has shown in the *Self after Post-Modernity*, quoting Mark Johnson, "Narrative is not just an explana-

22. Taylor, *Secular Age*, 545.

23. Much of the tension in Protestant theology between justification and sanctification would be resolved if, instead of seeing one as a status and the other as a story, or each as a status, we understood salvation as always a story and that status (justified and sanctified) is a reification that serves dogmatic interests, but not those of worship and mission.

tory device, but is actually constitutive of the way we experience things."[24] As importantly for the evangelist, "Narrative is also an indigenous feature of human action, providing the context and horizon for the "emplotment" of the multiple activities of the self against the backdrop of a tradition of communicative practices."[25]

This suggests that we may understand narrative as both entering into the narrative of God's reign and telling and enacting that story as the story of one's life: "Communicative praxis is both a discursive and non-discursive affair, implicating and constituting the self as once speaking and acting subject, texturing the genealogy of self-formation as an adventure, both in discourse and in action."[26] In this light, we can begin to see how the whole life of the church will look for those points at which human stories intersect and connect to the story of God's reign.

Example

To see how this might work in relation to the problem of insufficient—or even misguided—human stories, we can turn to the first chapter of *The Silmarillion*, which is a prelude to J. R. R. Tolkien's novels *The Hobbit* and *The Lord of the Rings*. Tolkien imagines that creation extends from the realm of God to a world of creatures in one contiguous set of islands surrounded by a cosmic sea. He then tells the neo-mythical story of how in the process of singing the earth into being, the chorus of angels is subtly led astray. Their song is distorted until it creates a world bent in on itself rather than extending toward the realm of its transcendent creator. This world appears complete, and everywhere on its surface leads to everywhere else, so it has the appearance of integrity and coherence.

It is, like our earth, a globe. It is Taylor's immanent frame. The meaning that humans weave for themselves in this world, even at their noblest, fall back in on themselves. All human quests curve back on their origin; they are inevitably less than what we as humans hoped them to be.[27] These are, of course, important themes running through the entire *Lord of the Rings* trilogy.

---

24. Schrag, *Self after Postmodernity*, 23.

25. Schrag, *Self after Postmodernity*, 41.

26. Schrag, *Self after Postmodernity*, 75

27. Tolkien, *Silmarillion*, 3–12.

Without recourse to biblical stories that have become sullied (if not rendered entirely powerless) by having been caught up in the long, fruitless modern debates between scientists and biblicists, Tolkien offers an account of the world in which we live. It is mythical, like the story of the fall in the Bible, but not burdened by a failed effort to place it within a scientific framework. Rather, like all good narrative, it skillfully invites the reader into a fictional universe that turns out in important respects to have features that map onto our own experience. It opens the possibility for a new self-emplotment that recognizes the "bent" context of human life and the false horizons that distort our personal stories.

The seeker after such resources may recognize significant points through this narrative (and, more particularly, through the characters of *The Lord of the Rings* who are more immediately human-like than those in the opening of the *Silmarillion*). All journeys bend back on themselves, and they are never able to reach a point from which there is a glimpse of the larger context of the story. The reversal in which the person abandons the limitations of being the center toward which meaning flows to become a pilgrim seeking God's rule may occur when he or she is caught up in a story that exposes the bent nature of our world and reorients the reader toward a transcendent end.

As important as the stories of Lewis, Tolkien, and Williams are, the worlds of contemporary science fiction and fantasy are stories set in a "wider ecumenism." While the greatest forms of art all draw people into a story, these emerging genres of fantasy and science fiction are more reflective of the contemporary experience of a hyper-pluralism. When Bilbo and Frodo leave the Shire, or when the children enter into Narnia, they experience something like discovering a different culture, if not walking among alien gods.

Rather than the formulations of dogmatic structures that offered so much appeal in modernity, the evidence that demands a verdict in our time is the story that draws people out of themselves and their finite worlds. C. S. Lewis, who characterized himself as the "last old Western man," must have understood that *Mere Christianity* would neither outlive nor reach as many people as *The Lion, the Witch, and the Wardrobe*. And Tolkien's *The Lord of the Rings* has probably done as much to create the conditions for faith than any conventional apologetic works.

Evangelism in the greater ecumenism may need to become a process of standing at the doors opened by the masters of story-telling and offering to tell one more story—one through which God speaks more explicitly. It is a story in which there is a shift in focus from the human actors to the divine context of their lives and thus the framework for real human authenticity. It is a story that has formed a community that reenacts the shift from a human story to a divine story continually, not only in worship but also in its mission to the world. We find a community in which we cannot reduce character to characteristics but as continually revealed and discovered in the dynamic of choice and action. The Fellowship of the Ring that lives beyond the book and outside the theater, of the Jedi Knights that are not found in a galaxy far, far away but here on earth, of the kings and queens of Narnia living out their gracious reign in a small town in Texas, a struggling urban center, or a white-flight suburb. Put another way, we discover a story that moves from myth into history while continually keeping touch with its transcendent dimension, in short, in the story of the Bible.

This insight takes us back to the problem of revisionist readings of the Bible. The failure of modernity with regard to the Bible is actually a twofold revisionism. As Abraham identifies, one aspect of this failure was the liberal reading of the Bible as a collection of stories disclosing the shape of human faith rather than the story of God's relationship with creation. This failure led to the kind of pluralism discussed in Abraham's chapter on the wider ecumenism.

Yet there is another aspect of revisionism at play in modern understandings of the Bible. It is found among Christians who believe that revelation is manifest in dogma; who reflexively read out of the narrative either an inappropriate synthesis or insufficient precipitate of doctrine that can be constructed into a systematic accounting of God's nature. In this, it fails to recognize that the underlying logic of the Bible as a whole is *narrative* rather than *propositional*. This form of revisionism, shaped by Greek culture and deeply constrained by modernity, doesn't recognize that *truth is the experience of lived coherence with God's story* expressed, in part, through—but not constituted by—systematically organized statements about reality.

Even at its best, propositional doctrine is a form of reverse engineering that tries to describe schematically what God has revealed in the living, moving, and changing voice in the Bible. And so, while it seeks to preserve the revelatory character of the Bible, it does so in a way that undermines evangelism in the greater ecumenism of multiple quests for meaning. It forecloses on the kind of evangelistic conversation in which stories might begin to intersect one another and conversions become possible because it puts the Bible immediately at odds with any set of beliefs that appear incongruent with whatever doctrinal formulation is extant. With regard to the Bible, it directs the reader into a process of analysis, of operating on the text rather than being drawn into its story. It focuses on a *change of mind* and even a *change of heart* without necessarily leading to a *change of narrative* and, hence, way of living.

Therefore, if we are reading the Bible as revealed doctrine, there is no point of conversation between Christians and Muslims regarding Jesus, even though both recognize him as a preeminently important figure. Christian beliefs precipitated out into the creeds from the Bible contradict traditional Islamic doctrine about Jesus precipitated out from the Qur'an.

Yet the stories of Jesus in both the Bible and the Qur'an are vastly richer than either Christian or Islamic doctrine. Muslims themselves remain fascinated with Jesus as the chief character in any number of stories from the Qur'an. As a result, evangelism among Muslims may take place—and has, in the experience of this author—at the intersection of the stories of Jesus and their own individual stories.

Beyond merely being narrative, I would argue that we best understand the Bible as the autobiography of God. The logic of the Bible is the logic of characters (primarily God) whose identities God reveals in the decisions they make in a series of increasingly consequential crises. At the center of its story, the Bible leads us through the series of these crises that God has faced in relation to that part of his creation called humanity. We know who God is because of what God does when faced with the behavior of God's people as they "act out" their freedom and stewardship. In telling us how God has responded to these crises, we learn more and more about how God will respond.

Therefore, God in the Bible is not some metaphysical construct. God does not primarily possess characteristics; God has and is a character. The reign of God in the Bible is not so much a place or state of being as it is what occurs when God reigns. It is why initiation into the reign of God is not a movement from one domain to another or from one set of beliefs to another, so much as it is moving from one narrative to another. It is quintessentially responding to the invitation of Jesus Christ to become his follower and thus making one's life story a story of living in God's-always-enacted-and-never-static reign. It is to become a pilgrim, both guided by and moving toward God.

When we understand ourselves in this way, and likewise understand our fellow human beings in this way, then the greater ecumenism looks different. It does not consist of religions or resources, but of *characters*. Of all these characters, the most consequential are those who prove to be witnesses, who keep pointing us again back into the story of God's rule. From beginning to end, we expect to find signs of God's presence as our own pilgrimage progresses, even as we rebel against it. We expect to experience contestation (not least within ourselves) as we seek to be faithful followers of the Christ. The greater ecumenism, then, is the much bigger stage and far greater cast of characters. The task of the evangelist in this epic is to be the witness who is constantly aware of other witnesses, the guide who keeps the traveler ever focused on the signs of God's realm, and the one who speaks of those places where God is most evident. This is how our "pathways" converge with the story of the Bible and the life of the church as we come to know God in Jesus Christ.

Chapter Ten

The Ministry of Evangelism

Ray Zirkel

Introduction

WHILE OTHER CONTRIBUTORS IN this volume have focused on the significance and impact of *The Logic of Evangelism* from a North American perspective, I would like to add a slightly different voice to the conversation. Having been introduced to the book's major proposals as a seminary student in the early 1990s, it wasn't until after spending several years of ministry with the Evangelical Methodist Church in Costa Rica that I was able to grasp a fuller understanding of many of Abraham's proposals and their potential beyond the North American church. As I approach over two decades of service in Costa Rica, I am convinced that the themes related to initiation into the kingdom of God are as relevant and necessary in other regions of the world as they are in the North America.

The following contribution is divided into two parts. The first is an overview of the chapter "The Ministry of Evangelism," with special attention given to Abraham's three general principles presented therein. The second portion is a reflection on how these principles have influenced the practice and theory of evangelism in the United States (to a lesser degree) and how they might be adopted to strengthen both the theory and practice of evangelism in other regions of the world, including Costa Rica.[1]

---

1 In using the Costa Rican Methodist church as my primary point of reference, I do not want to suggest that the observations made in this context will necessarily be as applicable in other regions of the world. My aim is simply to be another voice at the table and, in so doing, illustrate the extensive potential for the concepts/principles highlighted

Abraham begins the chapter on ministry by returning to the familiar theme of evangelism as either proclamation or church growth. He then makes an assertion which points to the corresponding relationship between theory and practice. More specifically, Abraham contends that what one believes regarding the nature of evangelism (what it is or isn't) will naturally lead to certain practices associated with one's corresponding belief. In turn, these practices will be evaluated according to their defined objectives and ultimately lead to the determination of success or failure in the practice of evangelism.[2]

Having made clear the critical role that one's concept of evangelism plays in his/her practice of the same, Abraham invites the reader to consider some of the potential outcomes flowing from his proposed concept of evangelism as initiation into the kingdom of God. In fact, he describes the chapter's aim as one in which the reader is invited to "explore the implications of my proposal for the ministry of evangelism."[3] With such an invitation, the reader senses that what follows will have both a degree of novelty and fluidity in the search for practical ways of incorporating the proposals into the life of the church.

Yet what follows is not the "new and improved" plan for evangelism. Abraham does not offer five easy steps to fill the pews. Nor does he share insights into the proper method of conducting altar calls. Instead, the author pauses and challenges the reader to a time of introspection. He makes a call for self-examination regarding one's own motives and desires for evangelism. In so doing, Abraham highlights a familiar obstacle present to contemporary Christ followers: the danger of losing one's passion for evangelism.[4] In referencing a letter from Wesley to his preachers, Abraham suggests that such a loss can present itself in a multitude of forms, ranging from focusing on numbers more than individuals, fixating on finances rather than outreach, or even on one's own comfort above sacrifice.[5] In each case, these conditions represent the fading of a flame that once burned bright to reach others with the good news of the gospel. In offering this consideration, the author begins an account of the ministry of evangelism

within the work. Certainly, additional global voices are welcome and would bring further insight to future reflections on Abraham, *Logic of Evangelism*.

2. Abraham, *Logic of Evangelism*, 164.

3. Abraham, *Logic of Evangelism*, 164.

4. Abraham, *Logic of Evangelism*, 165.

5. Abraham, *Logic of Evangelism*, 165.

not with a program or even a reference to his own proposal, but in raising an indirect yet penetrating question to the individual reader and the greater church at large: how strong does the fire burn within? Is there a passion to share the love of God in Christ Jesus with others? Without such a passion, the church has surely lost its way and is no longer being faithful to its apostolic mission.[6]

As the chapter continues, Abraham acknowledges that, in many sectors of the church, a genuine passion for evangelism remains readily evident. Nevertheless, he suggests that given the often-compartmentalized understanding of the practice of evangelism, passion and enthusiasm do not always burn with a constant flame.[7] While expressing his admiration for the fervor and energy on display, Abraham acknowledges a real need to channel such energy towards "activities that actually embody a responsible ministry of evangelism."[8]

Against the backdrop of what could be referred to as "event centered" evangelism, the author ultimately extinguishes the hopes of those still searching for a single program, activity or campaign, as he affirms that such a program would be completely "at odds with his basic vision" of evangelism as "a polymorphous ministry."[9] A "one size fits all" understanding of evangelism, he asserts, is in fact unworthy of the Christian gospel, subject to limiting human innovation and one's reliance upon divine inspiration.[10] Thus, instead of a "program" for the ministry of evangelism, Abraham moves the conversation in a new direction as he offers several "guiding principles" for such a ministry.

The first principle which Abraham proposes is the development of an awareness of the rule and reign of God within the community of faith. He contends that regardless of how strong the passion to participate in evangelism might be, the fundamental truth is that "the primary agent in all evangelism is God, and the ultimate objective (of evangelism) is to see people introduced to and grounded in the kingdom of God as it is manifested

---

6. Abraham, *Logic of Evangelism*, 167.

7. Few who have studied or participated in evangelism campaigns can deny the remarkable energy and passion readily evident prior to (and especially during) the event—and Costa Rica is no different. Yet once completed, the same energy and fire tend to all but disappear until the next "event" comes to town!

8. Abraham, *Logic of Evangelism*, 167.

9. Abraham, *Logic of Evangelism*, 167.

10. Abraham, *Logic of Evangelism*, 167.

in history."[11] Worded in a slightly different way: God must be allowed to be God and recognized as such. Where does that recognition take place? Abraham suggests that it is in the context of worship, where the reign of God is recognized and affirmed and one's willingness to acknowledge and celebrate the rule and reign of God is ultimately tested.[12]

Using the quality of worship as a means of measuring his first guiding principle, Abraham contends that where worship is "weak" (due to a misplaced focus), the rule and reign of God is also weakened. Under such conditions, he acknowledges evangelism, too, will suffer the consequences and often fail.[13] Conversely, Abraham proposes that where the reality of God is acknowledged through worship properly construed, where disciples acknowledge the reign of God in their midst, participants will experience the joy, wonder, and mercy that will sustain the ministry of evangelism over extended periods of time. Furthermore, such worship will even help to safeguard the ministry of evangelism from becoming a burden or obligation only to be completed by a sense of duty.[14] Finally, Abraham concludes this section by recognizing a self-sustaining element flowing from the link between evangelism and worship. He affirms that while some communities of faith may experience a lull in their sense of wonder and grace during worship, through hearing the voices of new believers and the corresponding sense of awe and mercy, the church itself is "reevangelized" and a sense of recognition of God's reign is revived anew in the worship setting.[15]

The second guiding principle Abraham offers is an update on the meaning of proclamation. The author begins with a reminder regarding the nature of the gospel itself. The Good News is content specific and has as its focus the acts of God in history through the life, death, and resurrection of Jesus Christ. This is the message which must be proclaimed. Yet for Abraham, ideally, this is not something to be done so much in a formal "institutional" setting but rather in an informal "marketplace" environment, where believers "gossip the gospel" with those around them.[16]

Abraham continues to develop the principle of proclamation through several additional observations. First, he contends that true proclamation

11. Abraham, *Logic of Evangelism*, 168.

12. Abraham, *Logic of Evangelism*, 168.

13. Abraham, *Logic of Evangelism*, 168.

14. Abraham, *Logic of Evangelism*, 168.

15. Abraham, *Logic of Evangelism*, 170.

16. Abraham, *Logic of Evangelism*, 171.

must leave room for a response. The evangelist cannot simply be content to "get the word out." Ideally, such a response would be one of faith and repentance. Nevertheless, regardless of the outcome, providing an opportunity to respond affirms the evangelist's conviction that he/she is engaged in a real conversation with other human beings for whom Christ died.[17] Second, Abraham cautions the reader of sliding into a mechanical approach to proclamation. To avoid such a pitfall, he entreats them to saturate the entire evangelistic process (including proclamation) in prayer, regardless of the persuasiveness, sincerity, or integrity of the one sharing the good news. Through prayer, the evangelist is reminded of his/her total dependence upon the inward and mysterious work of the Holy Spirit who "convicts the world of sin, of righteousness and of judgment."[18] Abraham's third observation considers the context of the hearer. Following the apostle Paul's words of becoming "all things to all men" (1 Cor 11:22), Abraham stresses the need for evangelists to both present the gospel without compromise and simultaneously become students of culture to "meet the people where they are, drawing them into the orbit of the kingdom taking up all that is valid, true, and God-given in the native culture."[19] Finally, the author concludes his discussion of proclamation with a familiar reminder regarding one's intentions. Although the evangelist's proclamation makes room for a response, even when it is bathed in prayer and takes the context of the hearer seriously, it is not yet evangelism. These and other related elements only form a part of true evangelism when they are carried out with the intention of initiation into the Kingdom of God. All other motives (raising money, altar calls, etc.) ultimately fall short of initiating new believers into the Kingdom by themselves and therefore cannot be considered evangelism.[20]

Abraham's third general principle for the ministry of evangelism directs the reader to the heart of his thesis and an understanding of evangelism as initiation into the Kingdom of God through the reestablishment of the catechumenate. According to the author, to ensure that all six dimensions of initiation (conversion, baptism, morality, the creed, spiritual gifts, and spiritual disciplines) are completed, the need arises for the creation of a public institution like the catechumenate. Given that each of the six areas are in one way or another related to each other, Abraham is not nearly as

17. Abraham, *Logic of Evangelism*, 171.

18. Abraham, *Logic of Evangelism*, 172.

19. Abraham, *Logic of Evangelism*, 172.

20. Abraham, *Logic of Evangelism*, 173.

concerned about the order in which they are presented as that they are given balanced and full attention throughout the initiation process.[21] The complete path of initiation is portrayed as one to be celebrated through intentionality and firmness, making use of the great "ceremonial treasures" in the life of the church. In addition, Abraham underscores the fact that through each of the six dimensions, one is reminded of God's original acts in history through Jesus Christ and entry into His kingdom is repeatedly recognized as the principal motive for each practice.[22]

Abraham moves on to make several more observations related to the overall ministry of evangelism. For example, he identifies current structures where elements of initiation are currently in place and which could be easily modified and incorporated into the larger process (e.g., confirmation, covenant groups, retreats, etc.). Abraham encourages the evangelist to take the process of initiation seriously while simultaneously not prolonging it indefinitely. Furthermore, he acknowledges that, in certain circumstances, the need may arise for a "calling to account" of those not willing to commit to the initiation process. The author continues with a necessary reminder that even the completion of the initiation process does not guarantee permanent entry into the kingdom. Nevertheless, he provides examples which illustrate that where such initiation is given its rightful place (the early Church and early Methodism) the likelihood of entry into the Kingdom significantly increases.[23]

Abraham concludes the chapter by raising one final set of related questions: if evangelism is so critical to the mission of the church, how should one go about his/her business in the church? How is evangelism best understood compared to other ministries? How does it relate to "everything else" in the life of the Christian community? Is it primary or secondary?[24]

Though committed to his proposal, Abraham does not hesitate in asserting that the Kingdom and only the Kingdom of God is primary. All other practices, ministries, etc., are secondary in nature compared to the reign of God. Evangelism is important solely because it initiates people into the Kingdom.[25] Abraham continues by suggesting that evangelism is perhaps best understood as a porch in relation to the ultimate objective of leading

21. Abraham, *Logic of Evangelism*, 175.
22. Abraham, *Logic of Evangelism*, 177.
23. Abraham, *Logic of Evangelism*, 179.
24. Abraham, *Logic of Evangelism*, 181.
25. Abraham, *Logic of Evangelism*, 182.

"lives of love and mercy" within the house. The porch cannot be considered equivalent to life within the kingdom but rather serves as a means to the ultimate end. Notwithstanding, where evangelism (the porch) is understood as the gathering, establishing, and grounding of persons in the faith, it is of critical importance for enabling persons to actually "enter into the house" and remain in a kingdom characterized by justice and love.[26]

Costa Rica as Context

Having highlighted Abraham's three general principles for the ministry of evangelism, we can now move to consider how these have influenced (or potentially could influence) the concept of evangelism and related practices within the broader church and the Costa Rican Methodist Church in particular.

From the outset, we should be made aware that *The Logic of Evangelism* has not been translated into Spanish and therefore few direct links can be found between the specific chapter and related theories/practices of evangelism in Costa Rica. Nevertheless, Abraham's subsequent work on the subject, e.g., *The Art of Evangelism* published in Spanish in 1993 (*El Arte de la Evangelización*) has been used as a reference work while teaching at the Evangelical Methodist Seminary in Costa Rica. In addition, this edition has been widely distributed among Methodist students and pastors throughout the country. Finally, it should be noted that the Evangelical Methodist Church of Costa Rica has been blessed to have Abraham teach courses on numerous occasions to both clergy and laity. Regardless of the "official" theme of the course, given his commitment to evangelism, it is highly likely that certain elements related to the practice have invariably "seeped through" other courses and influenced the Methodist community in Costa Rica. As suggested above, it is my intention to acknowledge the impact some of these principles have made within the church in Costa Rica and highlight still other areas where they have either met with greater resistance or have yet to make any significant impact.

26. Abraham, *Logic of Evangelism*, 184.

Evangelism in Costa Rica

For the missiologist, global church historian, church planter, or even the "veteran mission trip member," reports of expanding growth among Protestant churches in much of Latin American will come as no surprise. In his major work on the subject, *Tongues of Fire*, David Martin documents the dramatic rise of Protestantism in Latin America at the end of the last century and most notably among Pentecostal denominations.[27] The Protestant church in Costa Rica is no exception to this trend. For example, a 1983 survey found that 8.6 percent of the population were members of Protestant churches. In 2000, the percentage had grown to roughly 16 percent and by 2012, a Gallup poll placed the numbers at nearly 23 percent.[28] While many of the churches leading this historic increase represent traditional Pentecostal denominations, the Evangelical Methodist Church has also witnessed a major period of growth over the past fifteen years. For example, Clifton Holland estimates that Methodist membership in 2001 was close to 5000 persons.[29] Amazingly, recent internal estimates (2017) indicate a profound increase within the denomination, as current membership approaches 25,000.[30]

Due at least in part to the large Pentecostal influence, a great majority of Protestant churches in Costa Rica are theologically conservative and the Evangelical Methodist church would be included among them. Evangelism remains both a familiar concept and a promoted practice within much of the Protestant church, including the Evangelical Methodist Church. Having been blessed to serve in several leadership roles within this church for over two decades, I can affirm that evangelism is recognized as a vital part of the general ministry of the Methodist denomination. The church's commitment to this ministry is exemplified in the appointment of two pastors to serve as full-time evangelists throughout the country. There is no need to "apologize for evangelism" within the Costa Rican Methodist church as numerous members refer to the Great Commission (Matt 28:18–20), as "the motivation" for their evangelistic endeavors and eagerly await the next programed event.

---

27. Martin, *Tongues of Fire*, 51–52.
28. Holland, "Public Opinion Polls."
29. Holland, "Table of Estimated Size."
30. Igelsia Evangelica Metodista de Costa Rica, "iglesiametodistacr.com."

Does The Logic of Evangelism Fit in Costa Rica?

When considering the theological landscape in Latin America, we might conclude the initial anticipated reaction to Abraham's proposal regarding evangelism favorable. Yet upon further examination, what we discover is that for many in Costa Rica (including those within the Methodist Church), evangelism has most often been understood as and limited to "soul winning." The church has placed a priority on providing people with making an immediate decision to Christ, with concentration of efforts on preaching campaigns, sharing tracts, altar calls, etc. In contrast, Abraham's proposal of evangelism—understood as a "polymorphous process" directed toward initiation into the Kingdom of God—greatly extends the parameters of the practice. Initially, at least, we would expect a high level of resistance to such a proposal, either for not being considered "real" evangelism or for representing a host of unnecessary practices.

Therefore, even though Abraham's proposals represent a definite shift from historic and even current practices in evangelism, the initial steps towards a change in concept and practices are not as distant as we might imagine. While most within the Methodist Church of Costa Rica might have difficulty labeling the "whole package" of initiation as evangelism, in practice, a great number of persons already affirm Abraham's three general principles and to these we now turn our attention.

In addition, though we would be hard pressed to identify a formal conceptual link (the first general principle) between worship and evangelism within Costa Rican Methodism, few members would deny the fact that their worship experiences celebrate with joy and power the fullness of Christ's lordship in the church and God's mighty acts of redemption. Nor would many question the strong presence of the Holy Spirit indwelling believers and bestowing upon them gifts of various kinds. God's Spirit is being poured out in worship!

Therefore, we may ask that if the worship "component" is both conceptually and practically a reality within much of the Costa Rican Methodist church, we may also ask, what is the case regarding Abraham's second principle of proclamation?

As indicated earlier, a perceived "need" for evangelism among Costa Rican Protestants is not lacking. Yet, when comparing Abraham's second principle to the actual concepts and practices of the church, we can identify certain similarities. For example, while Abraham maintains a place for formal presentations (e.g., preaching services, campaigns, etc.), he also suggests that proclamation is best rooted in the informal settings emerging from organic relationships.[31] In his work *El Crecimiento y La Deserción de la Iglesia Evangélica Costarricense*, Costa Rican pastor and researcher Jorge Gomez identified a shift towards such a relational model of evangelism. According to Gomez, evangelism through existing friendships was found to be the preferred method for slightly more than 50 percent of those surveyed.[32] Nevertheless, while this might have been the "preferred" method, further data from the same study suggests that the actual number of persons engaged in relational evangelism may be somewhat lower. For example, 25 percent of those surveyed indicated a belief that evangelism is a ministry reserved only for the highly trained specialist and nearly 42 percent of those who were born within the Protestant church felt little or no need to evangelize at all.[33]

When engaged in "semi-relational" methods of evangelism (e.g., door to door), the reviews are mixed as to how culturally sensitive Christ followers in Costa Rica have approached the subject. In one scenario, for example, local Christians evangelize door to door by bringing along at least one "foreigner" as a conversation starter. Then, after presenting a gospel tract (and taking full advantage of Costa Rican hospitality and abhorrence to even the slightest degree of conflict), the foreign "guest" will ask the host for a response. Not wanting to offend their "guest," the host often responds with the perceived desired response (accepting Christ). Yet as many pastors have shared with this missionary/professor, when further follow up is given to these new "believers," the most often repeated response is, "Oh, I only said what they wanted me to, so they would leave my house!" One need not linger too long in contemplating similar evangelism practices before concluding that Abraham's call for a deeper understanding of context and culture is not simply a relevant word of advice but rather a critical word of warning for future cross-cultural endeavors.

Within the Evangelical Methodist Church, the practice of proclamation has taken on a variety of forms which often correspond to Abraham's model. Beyond the more formal ministries (the two full-time evangelists), the equipping of laity and clergy for personal evangelism through literature, seminars, and workshops has been a common practice.[34] In most congrega-

---

31. Abraham, Logic of Evangelism, 171.

32. Gómez V., *El Crecimiento*, 113.

33. Gómez V., *El Crecimiento*, 89, 113.

34. Eddie Fox has conducted several conferences on evangelism within the Methodist

tions, an invitation is given for those who wish to respond to the message in faith and repentance. Perhaps the least visible element is the link between proclamation and initiation and to that third dimension.

Interlude

Before considering Abraham's third general principle from the Costa Rican angle, I would like to return briefly to a critical question with respect to the process of initiation into the kingdom of God: what are some notable developments related to initiation that have occurred since *The Logic of Evangelism* was published? That is, how has the rise or the implementation of a catechumenate been helpful?

In response, I share two positive advancements. First, in *The Art of Evangelism*, Abraham again addresses the original six components of initiation in an even clearer and more detailed manner. The work includes an outline, a course description complete with chapter titles, suggested time periods for each class, and a host of practical suggestions which significantly advanced the "catechumenate" ball down the field.[35]

Though moving from the theory of a catechumenate to a course outline was a positive step, even more instructive was the collaborative effort between Abraham and members of First United Methodist Church in Uvalde, Texas, in the development of a complete curriculum entitled *Basic Christianity: A Contemporary Catechumenate* (1990). This material closely followed the outline included in *The Art of Evangelism*, but went even further in providing a leader's guide, student manual, audio/visual aids, detailed time suggestions, a training event for leaders, and two highly experiential sessions, including a covenant service to conclude the 12-week course.[36] From FUMC Uvalde, *Basic Christianity* was shared with neighboring congregations, and within two years, the catechumenate was being taught in several large churches in Texas—including University UMC in San Antonio, Highland Park UMC in Dallas, and First UMC in Houston.

Church of Costa Rica and numerous books including *Faith Sharing* (1996) and *Let the Redeemed of the Lord Say So* (1999), which have been distributed throughout the church.

35. Abraham, *Art of Evangelism*, 107–11.

36. As a member of the Uvalde church at the time, I had the blessing of witnessing staff and lay members passionately develop this course first for use within the Uvalde congregation. The effects were life altering for many participants as they came to a new and fuller awareness of the meaning of their faith.

In subsequent years, training courses for the catechumenate reached as far as Lake Junaluska, and *Basic Christianity* was even translated into German and finally into Russian.[37] Though unfortunately no longer in print, many of *Basic Christianity*'s former teachers and students continue to use the essential content of the course in new member classes and small group discipleship gatherings as a resource of rooting and grounding persons in the kingdom of God.[38]

Once back in Costa Rica, the question arises whether anything resembling "catechism" could ever find success in such a predominantly Roman Catholic country. On further analysis, however, nomenclature would be one of the easiest obstacles to overcome. What appears to be significantly more problematic would be the conceptual challenge of understanding initiation as a critical component of evangelism itself. This obstacle is further exposed in Gomez's investigation as he observes that for many Costa Ricans, the act of conversion is understood as an entirely transformative and instantaneous experience. For example, when asked if God completely transforms one's feelings, emotions, and mind in the moment of conversion, 60 percent responded in the affirmative.[39] Further revealing in the study was the fact that a significant number of persons closely associated conversion with an anticipated future full of physical and economic prosperity.[40] Even if the "health and wealth" misconceptions are laid aside, the persistent belief that conversion not only brings with it instant eternal security but also the complete transformation of one's character, knowledge, and emotions. This notion of conversion represents a formidable conceptual obstacle to overcome. We can only imagine that a natural response to the offer of the catechumenate might be, "What for? I've already been converted!"

Despite the apparent difficulty in launching a catechumenate within the Protestant church, information acquired through Gomez's research clearly signals a need for a similar style component to evangelism in Costa Rica. One phase of this study illustrated that fewer than one in five new believers had received any type of follow-up or discipleship following their conversion experience. Often, these persons grew weary of the lack of oversight and simply slipped out the back door.[41] Illustrative of the lack of disci-

---

37. Abraham, *World Mission in the Wesleyan Spirit*, 76.

38. Barber, Dori. Personal Interview. 29 January 2018.

39. Gómez V., *El Crecimiento*, 103.

40. Gómez V., *El Crecimiento*, 108.

41. Gómez V., *El Crecimiento*, 92.

pleship, the investigation also revealed a lack of understanding concerning the basic theological/historical tenets of the faith as found in the creeds. No doubt this was also due in part to the fact that among the "evangelists" who were interviewed, nearly 35 percent didn't feel the need to share about the historic work of Christ's life, death, and resurrection. Instead, they had "evangelized" by sharing their testimonies of personal experiences within the church.[42] According to the same investigation, fundamental truths related to the moral dimension of the faith were in short supply. When asked why they had left the Protestant church, the most common response among former members was due to their own moral failure. Gomez concludes that new Christians didn't feel capable of living up to the standards of the faith and opted to leave rather than remain in a frustrated and often lonely condition.[43] Addressing the issue with an even wider lens, Justo Gonzalez observes that the Latin American Protestant church has frequently stressed the importance of "believing in Jesus Christ and thus being saved," yet has not dedicated the same effort or energy to the implication of belief: "obedience to Christ." "In other words," he writes "justification continues on into sanctification" and where sanctification is absent, the result is a "truncated gospel."[44]

As I consider the possibilities of a catechumenate for Costa Rican Methodism, I am encouraged that each of the six themes of initiation are currently covered as a part of our seminary curriculum. Hopefully, they will also be added to our new members classes and thus be accessible to an even broader section of the church. Currently, there is a greater appreciation for the concept of grounding within the church than ever before. Small group "classes meetings" have recently been formed, and members throughout the country have access to spiritual gifts inventories. What remains is the incorporation of these components into the very fiber of evangelism itself. Though perhaps known by a different name, with such a process in place, the hope is for generations of Costa Rican Christians to move ever closer to knowing and living under God's rule and His ultimate reign throughout the country and to the very ends of the earth.

42. Gómez V., *El Crecimiento*, 107.

43. Gómez V., *El Crecimiento*, 85.

44. González, *Juan Wesley*, 108–9.

Future Work/Conclusion

Though not originally directed to a global audience, *The Logic of Evangelism*—and, more specifically, the principles contained therein—have arrived on distant shores. In some instances, this has been the direct result of Abraham's own ministry. Yet it is my suspicion that a far greater number of those influenced by his proposals are represented by second and third generation Christians who themselves were initiated into the faith in a manner consistent with Abraham's positions. It remains to be seen what the longer-term impact of these positions and proposals will have in places such as Costa Rica. Nevertheless, the need for the union of proclamation with initiation has been evidenced. Just as the gospel itself is applicable across all cultural divides, so too is the persistent call for a faith which is firmly grounded through initiation, regardless of cultural context. Further cross-cultural investigations along these lines would be one manner of continuing the discussion. Additionally, the acquisition and updating of data similar to that found in Gomez's research would be extremely useful in evaluating the extent to which evangelistic practices have initiated new members into the kingdom.

Chapter Eleven

Evangelism and Modern Theology

Vaughn W. Baker

Introduction

MY RELATIONSHIP WITH WILLIAM J. Abraham began after he arrived at Perkins School of Theology in the 1980s. We both shared a conviction that the good news of the gospel needs to be communicated and that all persons need Christ; hence, we shared a deep interest in the practice of evangelism. The contributions found in this volume come from those who likewise have shared with Abraham a passion for mission, evangelism, and theology.

Methodist theologian David Lowes Watson notes that when it comes to current attitudes toward evangelism, the effect is two-fold: for laypersons the words *evangelism* or *evangelization*[1] evoke a response of embarrassment; for the clergy, the response is one of bewilderment.[2] Such embarrassment and bewilderment reflect similar attitudes found in the academy where such training takes place. It is a notable irony as universities and schools of theology are institutions that were once explicitly committed to educating practitioners to spread the gospel

For example, we can note the plaque to the entrance of Kirby Hall at Perkins where it states the mission of the seminary: "Having profound faith in the divinity of Jesus Christ; knowing God's guidance, His boundless love for mankind and great desire that all men shall be saved; and believing

---

1. In this essay, I will assume that the words "evangelism" and "evangelization" are synonymous.

2. Watson, "Church as Journalist," 57–74.

firmly in Christian education, we will give one hundred thousand dollars to Southern Methodist University for a theological building. Mr. & Mrs. R. Harper Kirby."[3] A similar statement also states: "The primary mission of Perkins School of Theology, as a community devoted to theological study and teaching in the service of the church of Jesus Christ, is to prepare women and men for faithful leadership in Christian ministry."[4] We may wonder why, given such affirmations in both 1925 and 2001, regarding the origin and mission of Perkins and SMU—why bewilderment, embarrassment, and perhaps even hostility toward evangelism should take place.

But Perkins is hardly alone in what I shall choose to call the missional "disconnect" in theological education (or the growing gap between institutional mission statements and current practice). An obvious example is Harvard University, founded in 1636 with the intention of establishing a school to train Christian ministers. In accordance with that vision, Harvard's "Rules and Precepts," adopted in 1646, stated (original spelling and Scriptural references retained):

> 2. Let every Student be plainly instructed, and earnestly pressed to consider well, the maine end of his life and studies is, to know God and Jesus Christ which is eternal life (John 17:3) and therefore to lay Christ in the bottome, as the only foundation of all sound knowledge and Learning. And seeing the Lord only giveth wisedome, Let everyone seriously set himself by prayer in secret to seeke it of him (Prov 2:3).

> 3. Every one shall so exercise himselfe in reading the Scriptures twice a day, that he shall be ready to give such an account of his proficiency therein, both in Theoreticall observations of Language and Logick, and in practical and spiritual truths, as his Tutor shall require, according to his ability; seeing the entrance of the word giveth light, it giveth understanding to the simple (Psalm 119:130).[5]

The motto of the University adopted in 1692 was, "Veritas Christo et Ecclesiae," which, translated from Latin, means, "Truth for Christ and the Church." This phrase was originally embedded on the shield of Harvard

---

3. This plaque was located in the previous "Kirby Hall," now part of the SMU Law School. It can now be found in the current Kirby Hall, located in the Perkins School of Theology, quadrangle where the new seminary campus was built in 1948.

4. Perkins School of Theology, "Perkins' Mission."

5. Harvard GSAS Christian Community, "Shield and Veritas History."

and is found on many buildings around campus, including the Widener Library, Memorial Church, and various dorms in Harvard Yard. Interestingly, the top two books on the shield face up while the bottom books face down. This configuration symbolizes the limits of reason and the need for God's revelation. With the secularization of the school, the shield now contains only the word, "Veritas," with three open books. Clearly, the institution has distanced itself from its founding evangelistic principles. Harvard's failure to "mind the gap" is not unique.

Another example of "missional disconnect" is Yale University. Established in 1701, Yale's mission was to educate Congregational ministers. It moved to New Haven in 1716 and changed its name to honor Elihu Yale. The purpose of the "renamed" school was "To plant and under ye Divine blessing to propagate in this Wilderness, the blessed Reformed, Protestant Religion, in ye purity of its Order and Worship."[6]

Students at Yale were required to "live religious, godly, and blameless lives according to the rules of God's Word, diligently reading the Holy Scriptures, the fountain of light and truth; and constantly attend upon all the duties of religion, both in public and secret." Prayer was a requirement. Furthermore, every student was instructed to "consider the main end of his study to wit to know God in Jesus Christ" and "to lead a Godly, sober life."[7] Like Harvard, Yale's founding had the spreading of the gospel of Jesus Christ and the making of disciples at its core. We can give similar accounts of many other colleges and universities that began as training centers for ministers of the gospel, along with a clear vision of what God was doing in the world, only to end up going another way.

Given the founding mission statements of both Harvard and Yale (and, much later, the Perkins School of Theology), we may wonder why evangelism has had to fight for its own existence and survival in the academy when it seems to fit hand-in-glove with the very conception and existence of these and other academic institutions. Indeed, were it not for evangelism, these institutions would not exist! Such bedrock affirmations, regarding both the content of the Christian faith and the need to spread that faith in order to see conversions take place and new believers initiated, were clearly a "given" when Harvard and Yale were founded. In other words, the secularization of the Christian academy has clearly taken place.

---

6. Harvard GSAS Christian Community, "Shield and Veritas History."

7. Graves, "Yale Founded to Fight Liberalism."

Such secularization in divinity schools and universities is now the setting where evangelism struggles to establish itself as a legitimate field of study.

The problem experienced today is that many God-called aspiring pastors, full of the fire of proclaiming the gospel of God, enroll at a United Methodist seminary wanting to preach the gospel; after three years of theological studies, they end up wanting to pursue a PhD and teach in seminary. Left to themselves, academic theological institutions tend to be self-serving and self-cloning. Such was my own experience, having heard and heeded the call of God to preach the gospel and spread the good news about Jesus. Instead, at Perkins I received another vision and was able to enter graduate school and teach.[8] Clearly, the academy is adept at reproducing itself. In fact, it would appear that graduate school admission, with an eye toward earning a PhD degree and entering a life-long career in teaching at a seminary, can prove seductive to a budding seminary student. Serving the interests of the academy, whatever those may be, needs to be subservient to serving the mission of the church. Seminaries are centrifugal by nature and not centripetal. Without the compelling mission of taking the gospel out into the world, it is doubtful the institutions previously mentioned would even exist, at least not in any recognizable form. One immediate result of the academy distancing itself from both its founding mission of evangelism and training church leaders for ministry, then, is that evangelistic training of church leaders is being handed over to the local church itself.

Not long after the publication of William J. Abraham's book, *The Logic of Evangelism*, I had my first encounter with what was becoming known as a "mega-church." It was in the spring of 1992 when I attended a church growth conference at the Community Church of Joy (ELCA) in Phoenix, Arizona, with Walt Kallestad.[9] It was there that I saw first-hand what kinds of ministry a very large church can do. Among the various speakers at the conference was Lyle Schaller, a United Methodist church growth author

8. In a 1977 Systematic Theology class, it was in visits with Professors John Deschner and later Schubert Ogden where I was encouraged to enter the PhD program in theology. It was David Lowes Watson, however, who led me to do a Doctor of Ministry in Evangelism, "not to abandon the field," and to be a practitioner of evangelism. The Polycarp Community, under the leadership of Professor Abraham, has helped me navigate a "middle way."

9. On February 28, 2016, Community Church of Joy (CCOJ) merged with Phoenix First Assembly of God, to form Dream City Church, Glendale. These two megachurches were also two large denominational churches, Evangelical Lutheran and Assembly of God, but with a common vision, namely to "reach the Valley for Jesus Christ." See Dream City Church, "Our Story."

and strategist, who made the following statement: "Such evangelism conferences as this one, i.e., Community Church of Joy, would have at one time been held in a denominational seminary or school of theology. Or later, perhaps it would have been sponsored and hosted by a denominational board or agency. Recently, however, training and teaching evangelism and church growth has by and large been taken over by large mega-teaching churches such as we find ourselves in this evening."[10] Seminaries, rather than serving as training schools for clergy and other church leaders, have become for the most part graduate schools of religion. The disconnect of theological schools with evangelism results in increased isolation to mission. Indeed, it is ironic that many of our larger churches in America are led by pastors with no seminary degree at all. Such distancing of the academy from the church and its evangelistic imperative leads many to wonder what the point to theological training is. Is basic seminary education in the form of the Master of Divinity degree simply to serve as a "launching pad to a PhD degree"? We are left to ask, "What's it all about?"

A Voice in the Wilderness

Having taught the subject of evangelism at Perkins School of Theology Course of Study School, I began searching for books that dealt with the theology of evangelism. However, most material on the topic of evangelism in the 1980s dealt with practical matters of church growth, personal faith-sharing, evangelistic preaching, and the like. Very little could be found on the topic of evangelism beyond that of technique and skill development. My own struggle seemed to reflect what I once remembered hearing by Professor Roy Fish, who taught a variety of courses on evangelism and church renewal at the Southwestern Baptist Theological Seminary in Fort Worth, Texas. Immediately upon beginning his career as a seminary professor of evangelism, Dr. Fish was asked by fellow colleagues at the seminary if his evangelism was "theological." To which Dr. Fish replied, "Yes, it is! And may I ask 'Is your theology evangelistic?'"[11] While Fish's contribution to critical reflection on evangelistic practice was more practical than theoretical, he correctly discerned the tension which exists between respective seminary

10. Schaller spoke at an evening worship event that was part of the church growth conference in May 1992.

11. This account came from personal sharing in one of Dr. Fish's classes on evangelism in which I was enrolled, "Church Evangelism," 1977.

departments. Such tension between those who teach theology and those who teach evangelism would seem to be quite widespread and not limited to "liberal" or "mainline" schools of theology.

I ran across *The Logic of Evangelism* shortly after 1989, while teaching evangelism and serving full-time in the local church. The book gave me as good an answer as any to the questions cited earlier ("Is your theology evangelistic?" and "Is your evangelism theological?"). In the book, Abraham clearly united the two so long divided, knowledge and vital piety; he did so in a way that showed a "multidisciplinary nature of the discussion."[12] Abraham's theology was and is quite evangelistic, and his evangelism is likewise quite theological. Abraham was speaking the languages of church, the academy, and the larger society.

It has been said that there exist three audiences to whom the theologian speaks: the wider society, the academy, and the church.[13] Every theologian, therefore, addresses these audiences in critical reflection. The audience of the academy is where we employ fundamental or philosophical theology; the church is where we use symbolic or dogmatic language; and society is where we use practical or applied theology. *The Logic of Evangelism* addresses all three of these audiences in accomplishing its objective and in making good on modern theology. It is a book that speaks to the issue of the "missional disconnect" mentioned earlier and makes the Great Commission of the church a priority, as well as engaging in critical reflection upon the church's practice of evangelism in an academic setting. Abraham speaks the language of the academy, the church, and the larger culture and uses a kind of dexterity to move the church beyond the walls of the academy.

The Rift between Evangelism and Modern Theology

Abraham acknowledges why modern theologians have tended to ignore the issue of evangelism. First, much of what had been written on the topic tended to be heavy on the practice of evangelism. While the church has spoken to issues related to mission, ministry and church growth, we say little in terms of theological reflection: "Little of a really critical disposition that has sought to wrestle with the questions and the options open to the modern Christian community with respect to its activities in the field of

12. Abraham, *Logic of Evangelism*, 14.

13. Tracy, *Analogical Imagination*, 5.

evangelism."[14] The purpose of *The Logic of Evangelism* is to "make good on this deficiency."[15] Such an objective involved offering an account on the nature of evangelism and an articulation of the implications of that account for the practice of the church in the ministry of evangelism. While Abraham outlines what the church should do in this field, his "target" is that audience called the academy, arguing a case for taking evangelism "radically seriously" as a topic of theological inquiry. In so doing, he intends to move evangelism from the fringe of modern critical theology to the forefront. No doubt, the book speaks to the other audiences of church and society, but it is clear that the academy is the primary audience.

Abraham noted that other substantial authors on the subject of evangelism, such as Bryan Green and George Sweazey, were long on the practice but short on the critical reflection of evangelism.[16] What literature existed dealt more with the practice of evangelism, e.g., with technique and program. Abraham lists the reasons for such "paucity" of critical discussion about the theory and practice of evangelism, which include:

> 1. Assumption that Christianity is a part of the fabric of the west and therefore Christians don't have to evangelize.

> 2. The best intellectual efforts of the Christian community have been channeled into fields that either elbow out or inhibit serious engagement with the topic of evangelism.[17]

As a result, evangelism occupies a minor motif in practical theology. Abraham argues that practical theology itself is not a whole lot better off, being "at best construed as a rag-bag of bits and pieces on how to minister in the church, with highest honors paid to pastoral care, homiletics, liturgics, and administration; at worst it is the name given to a topic that no one knows how to define coherently but upon which everyone is an instant authority."[18]

---

14. Abraham, *Logic of Evangelism*, 1.

15. Abraham, *Logic of Evangelism*, 1.

16. Green, *Practice of Evangelism*, and Sweazey, *Effective Evangelism*.

17. Abraham, *Logic of Evangelism*, 5.

18. Abraham, *Logic of Evangelism*, 5. It bears noting how many teach courses on evangelism in our seminaries with little or no actual evangelistic experience. The norm seems to be to place faculty whose own doctoral study was in another field, i.e., church history, and have that instructor or assistant professor teach evangelism when there is no other place on the faculty for them to serve.

Abraham's argument is that "good work in evangelism depends crucially on sustained and independent research in a whole network of disciplines."[19] The conventions of the modern academic study of theology oppose such serious work in this field. Such a view renders suspect critical judgment and knowledge. Indeed, as Abraham notes, the whole theological enterprise itself is under assault, with precious time and energy given to address issues of fundamental viability, method, and issues regarding translation. Secularism and skepticism on a wide scale have left the church with many theologians who have "openly repudiated any interest in the conventional ministries of the church."[20] Both Anglican and Methodist churches have demonstrated less interest in the content of the Christian faith and instead have been devoted to questions regarding sources and norms. It is why we do not need to not get up our hopes. As Abraham states, we need to realize that given the academic context out of which we are operating, "our efforts are not going to be greeted initially with great enthusiasm"; he goes on to share that: "The whole ethos and content of twentieth-century theology to date has been incipiently hostile to tackling the fundamental issues raised by those interested in evangelism."[21] As a result, Abraham argues that it may take a generation before we can attain scholarly conversation essential in this area.

Abraham notes that what contributes to a climate of disinterest and apathy toward evangelism on the part of the academy is the linking of it with fundamentalist and conservative-evangelical Protestantism. Even dictionaries themselves confuse evangelism with evangelicalism. He notes that we should not be too surprised by this, given that "evangelicals have owned evangelism as a distinctive if not an exclusive characteristic of their contribution to modern Christianity."[22] Until recent years, evangelicals have demonstrated more interest in the practice of evangelism than theory, let alone critical self-reflection. Likewise, evangelicals are viewed as being more concerned about providing *apologia* for theories of biblical inspiration and distancing themselves from modern biblical criticism. It is in such a climate where memories of the fundamentalist-modernist controversy die hard and suspicions arise almost in knee-jerk fashion when one seeks to have evangelism as a field of critical refection to be taken seriously. His-

19. Abraham, *Logic of Evangelism*, 5.
20. Abraham, *Logic of Evangelism*, 6.
21. Abraham, *Logic of Evangelism*, 6.
22. Abraham, *Logic of Evangelism*, 6.

torical figures such as John Wesley, Jonathan Edwards, and Charles Finney notwithstanding, most modern figures in the evangelical movement—from D. L. Moody to the current televangelists at the time of the writing of this book—leave little to work with. Even in Billy Graham, as essential as he was in the founding of *Christianity Today* magazine and helping to forge and shape neo-evangelicalism, we do not find the sufficient theological development and definition needed to point the way forward. So where are we to look?

Abraham calls us to "take a hard look at what evangelism is, reflect seriously on what has gone wrong, and make some suggestions about how it might be pursued with integrity."[23] This key insight involves studying evangelism for its own sake. In engaging in critical reflection upon evangelism, we are forced to wrestle with the essence of Christianity: conversion, faith, and repentance. We also come to terms with the kingdom of God and the place of that kingdom in the ministry of Jesus. We are forced to think about the nature of baptism and Christian initiation, the relationship between the intellect and the emotions in Christian commitment. We also are drawn to examine how far the faith of the early centuries can be expressed in the modern world, including apologetics, and the rationality of theistic persuasion.[24] When approached in the right way, evangelism studies have a way of raising these issues. In other words, when we take evangelism seriously, as a legitimate field of study, we can see how the "tide lifts all the boats." In Abraham's proposal, we need to use both eyes, keeping one on the evangelistic activity of the church and the other on the relevant data and warrants that any scholar must draw upon. Much like the Apostle Paul, St. Polycarp, Jonathan Edwards, and John Wesley, Abraham believes that many of those who are engaged in evangelistic practice are today capable of engaging in serious critical theological reflection.

Abraham notes that as more studies in evangelism commence, many driven by experimentation in church growth, liberation theology, and Pentecostalism, we will find ourselves in a burgeoning field. We will see such an outburst as realization that the Spirit is doing something new and realize how Charles Wesley's sentiment of joining knowledge and vital piety holds fast to the notion of the "faith once delivered to the saints." These two aspects of faith are not opposites but rather are uniquely tied to the church's evangelistic imperative.

23. Abraham, *Logic of Evangelism*, 10.
24. Abraham, *Logic of Evangelism*, 11.

Chapter Twelve

Evangelism and Modernity

ANDREW D. KINSEY &
ANDREW G. WALKER

AT THE BEGINNING OF his chapter on "Evangelism and Modernity," William Abraham expounds on how the concept of modernity comes into play with respect to the ministry of evangelism. As an "essentially contested concept," modernity can cut along different lines, confusing categories and exposing biases. We can deploy the "modern" as a way to privilege our own positions versus other periods of history, especially periods which we may consider "out of date" or "ancient," or we may employ the term to render obsolete claims we want to discard. The modern is ever new but never arriving. Echoing C. S. Lewis, there is a kind of "chronological snobbery" built into the very concept of modernity itself as it seeks to displace what comes before.[1]

The reason Abraham spends time dealing with the concept of modernity is to share how the classical expression of the gospel he is advocating

---

1. Thanks to Steve Long for this insight on the ways modernity is always touting the new but never arriving; that is, modernity considers that everything we have done up to this point has not prepared us for this moment so that it must be rendered obsolete and discarded. The "new," however, never arrives. It is always delayed. We would also share how Long's view has definite affinities with C. S. Lewis's notion of "chronological snobbery." Lewis's use of the phrase "chronological snobbery," which he took from Owen Barfield, is apposite, for he argued that modern world assumes its contemporary philosophy and wisdom is always superior to the past. In fact, he did not mind if modern thinkers believed he amounted to an "old hat." Lewis's concern was what he took to be the false assumptions that ancient thinking was not merely old fashioned but invariably wrong; see Lewis, *Surprised by Joy*, 206.

can engage, if not thrive, in a modern world. As Abraham notes, the church has never relied on a sunny analysis of the culture it was seeking to evangelize to flourish. Indeed, the church has faced all kinds of opponents, intellectual, political, and otherwise. What the church must have is a kind of wherewithal amidst the acids of modernity to bring the healing power of the gospel to bear. It must possess a kind of intellectual backbone amidst a world that wants to distort the gospel from both within and without. Therefore, the challenge is to understand what modernity is and how it seeks to confound the ministry of evangelism.[2]

Abraham begins his analysis of the shift to a modern world by stating how we may prop up modernity against other periods of history. Bringing to light the work of Episcopal Bishop John Shelby Spong, Abraham shows how Spong's use of the concept of modernity can blind and lull us into thinking that, by living in a modern world, we can now throw off the prejudices of the premodern world as exclusivist and dogmatic, superstitious and unenlightened. Indeed, we can now walk in the light of modern worldview, of our new and superior present, not in the darkness our tribal pasts.[3]

Yet, as Abraham states, we need to walk carefully. There are other ways we may want to give an account of modernity; that is, there are insights from other fields we may want to glean as we seek clarify what modernity is. The first insight is sociological in nature, with the notion that (in the West, at least) we have seen an erosion of the influence of religion in public life over time, especially with respect to the way religion impacts political institutions and social mores. According to this account, religion becomes "relegated" to the private sphere, where matters of truth are "deregulated," if not delegitimized, to mere opinion. The fundamental ethos is impersonal as we figure out the ways in which we relate means and ends, mostly in the

---

2. Abraham, *Logic of Evangelism*, 202. It has been fifty years since the publication of H. Richard Niebuhr's highly influential book *Christ and Culture* (1967). Abraham does not really buy into two of the categories of Niebuhr's analysis: Christ above Culture and Christ against Culture. Abraham knows that evangelism is never free of culture and that we cannot understand Christ unless his story is translated into cultural idioms. While Abraham is happy to take on modern culture with the gospel, therefore, he knows from his own experience of being brought up in Northern Ireland the dangers of sectarianism (though Niebuhr was thinking more in terms of the Amish who refuse to conform to the mores of modern culture than the Amish *per se*). Abraham is all for transforming the culture through Christ (probably Niebuhr's personal choice), but his confidence in a robust evangelistic movement comes from the church and its tradition and not the cultural context of modernity.

3. Abraham, *Logic of Evangelism*, 186–87.

direction of the utilitarian and pragmatic, but rarely in terms of a "sacred canopy" where divine initiative constitutes social order.[4]

This relegation of religion to the private sphere, however, does not simply have societal consequences but also figures deeply into the ways the weighty matters of philosophy and natural sciences can also render as obsolete any kind of classical vision of evangelism where divine agency has a platform to pronounce and articulate claims to truth.[5] Here, the issues become more complex in terms of the relationship between cause and effect, but the outcome remains similar with respect to the ways the church carries out its mission: there is now a defensive posture in regards to the way in which the church expounds the gospel. Single out an area and we can note how the church has had to rejoin the claims of God's rule in Christ. For example, with the Copernican Revolution in the natural sciences, Christians have had to reconsider their doctrine of creation. No longer can Christians simply argue within a closed worldview of divine causality but now must take a whole new set of premises and propositions into consideration.[6] The list continues. With the rise of historical criticism in biblical studies, for instance, we can also see how assaults on God's activity in history would call into question the whole conception of divine action in *toto*, or how notions of divine inspiration and supernatural intervention in miracles would circumvent how we may conceive of the Holy Spirit's operations. In all areas, there is a new kind of contestation to classical Christian claims: human beings as created in the image of God? What about Darwin's account of human origins? Ordering of society? What is the nation-state and market economy? And so forth. These developments and more have had a profound impact on Christian theology.[7]

---

4. Abraham, *Logic of Evangelism*, 188. We are using Peter Berger's notion of the sacred canopy as a way to understand the way modernity has functioned to eclipse the supernatural or sacred claims of the gospel; see Berger, *Sacred Canopy*, 89–90.

5. Abraham, *Logic of Evangelism*, 189.

6. See John Wilson's chapter in this volume on the reconfiguring of Christian truth claims in regards to science and technology.

7. Abraham, *Logic of Evangelism*, 189. There are too many theories of modernity to mention, but one of the key resources to highlight with respect to how we have conceived of modernity is David Martin's *General Theory of Secularization*, where, depending on the country in mention, the way modernity unfolds entails a great deal on the way the relationship between church and state is conceived (Martin, *General Theory*, 15–17). It is far beyond this project to disentangle the issues here, but simply to note how, as Abraham later states in this chapter, modernity cuts in different directions: that moving in one direction to accommodate to one form of modernity, we shall find ourselves at odds

Therefore, we cannot ignore these and other challenges to the ministry of evangelism, whether directly or indirectly. We simply cannot, according to Abraham, put our heads in the sand and stop addressing the effects that modernity poses to classical theism in general and Christian theism in particular. To be sure, the mission field in the West has shifted.[8] However, as Abraham notes, there is no need to retreat in fear. The church and its theologians can engage modernity to the hilt, not succumbing to the temptation that all theological efforts begin and end only in prolegomena, or in spending time spelling out and proffering possible objections to our claims before taking up the necessary questions of the church's mission.[9] Naturally, such a posture can lead to discouragement, for evangelism depends significantly on robust notions of divine revelation and agency. It is why having the central claims of the gospel sidelined is no small matter. Nor is it a small matter to see how modernity may serve as a kind of anxiety-producing agent. When theologians no longer can pronounce the gospel as traditionally conceived, the outcomes as to what form Christianity may take in the world can become confusing, both inside and outside the church.[10]

Think of Bultmann's program of "demythologizing the gospel" or Harvey Cox and Paul van Buren's response of the "secular city" and "secular

---

with another form. Hence, the need to proceed cautiously with regards to the ministry of evangelism (Abraham, *Logic of Evangelism*, 203). Abraham proposes to view modernity through a philosophical and sociological lens. It is important to stress, however, that Abraham is not anti-modern; he sees the skepticism built into the Enlightenment as a blessing to be cherished. As well as being Wesleyan, Abraham is a philosopher not afraid to counter fundamentalist or anti-foundationalist conservatives as well as modernist liberals.

8. Abraham brings to the fore the shifting landscape of Western culture, noting how Lewis's classical approach to the Christian faith can bring intellectual clarity and zeal (Abraham, "C. S. Lewis and the Conversion of the West," 12–17); see also Walker, *Enemy Territory*, 69–70. Walker utilizes Lewis's writings to comprehend the hidden ways that modernity seeks to undermine the gospel.

9. Abraham, *Logic of Evangelism*, 190.

10. Abraham engages on different fronts with respect to modern theology in this chapter. He aptly calls attention, for example, to the force of Karl Barth's theology but states that Barth's project really did not lead to a revitalization of evangelism (Abraham, *Logic of Evangelism*, 190). He also, of course, points out the evangelical nature of Rudolf Bultmann's program of demythologizing, but argues even it can dissolve the central claims of the gospel (Abraham, *Logic of Evangelism*, 191). Later, Abraham brings the work of J.C. Hoekendijk into the conversation and his famous *Church Inside Out*. Rightly, Hoekendijk puts forward wonderful proposals regarding evangelism. Sadly, he does not pursue them in an ecclesiological direction (Abraham, *Logic of Evangelism*, 194–95).

meaning of the gospel." Here, in many respects, were courageous attempts to navigate the challenges of secular modernity while holding onto vestiges of the gospel, always seeking, in good conscience, creative ways of making the gospel relevant, whether as a direct existential encounter with the gospel's *kerygma*, in calling forth decision (Bultmann), or as a way to influence the surrounding environs by joining God in the neighborhood and participating with folks inside and outside the church to better society, making the gospel accessible in modern language (Cox and van Buren). Abraham's use of these examples is telling as he comes to terms with the ministry of evangelism in the church and with the notion of evangelism as initiation into the kingdom of God. Coming to grips with modernity is no small feat.[11]

Perhaps this is the reason Abraham's use of Fred Brown's *Secular Evangelism* is illuminating, for we can see how Abraham, in keeping with his central argument throughout *The Logic of Evangelism*, wants to retain the classical content of the gospel in the face of modernity's effects (e.g., arguing for divine agency) while also advocating a strong but realistic evangelistic mission (e.g., relying on the internal logic of the gospel in God's rule).[12] As Abraham states, the modern age does not need to set the agenda for the church's missionary and evangelistic endeavors. The coming of God's kingdom in Christ is what constitutes the church's agenda. The reign of God is the focus of attention providing the theocentric horizon.[13] Where persons like Brown stumble is how, despite their best intentions and efforts, they fall prey, at some point, to the acids of modernity, gutting the substance of the gospel from within and raising questions as to what persons actually believe when they become Christian and involved in the ministry of the

---

11. Notwithstanding Bishop John A. T. Robinson's *Honest to God*, the "death of God" controversies, and "secular theologies," we may understand Abraham's approach here as avoiding the pitfalls into which many theologies fell in the 1960s. Though the attempts to relate the gospel to "modern" or "secular" man were commendable, Abraham contends, the effects of those attempts were short-sighted, as they left the church with little theological substance to level ongoing critiques of modern society, not to mention how they also left behind the crucial aspects of God's agency and the nature and mission of the church. It is why Abraham is cautious with the proposals Harvey Cox, Paul van Buren, and others brought to the table during this period (Abraham, *Logic of Evangelism*, 193). Placing Fred Brown's *Secular Evangelism* in this context also helps to make sense of what is at stake.

12. Abraham, *Logic of Evangelism*, 191, 204

13. Abraham, *Logic of Evangelism*, 193, 204–5.

church.[14] They forget that there *is* strong intellectual content to the gospel as initiation into God's rule and that, despite plausibility structures in the modern world that would seek to rule out talk of God's agency, there are realistic accounts as to the ways God works to engender more comprehensive visions of freedom than modernity supposedly offers.[15] To be sure, such accounts seem foolish in the eyes of the world as they do not fit neatly into the modern scientific or natural accounts of reality. But even here, the church need not fall into despair. The Holy Spirit is quite capable of providing the kind of deep faith which reveals to the heart what the heart truly seeks and needs.[16]

Despite the rhetorical flourishes of Brown's argument regarding divine action and despite the great sensitivity Brown brings to seeking meaningful ways of sharing the gospel with folks whose vocabulary may not reference God with the traditional language of Zion, Abraham notes how Brown's strategy, while tactically useful, remains stunted in its appeal to the moral and theological commitments a person needs to make on entering into the Christian life.[17] Surely, Brown is correct in comprehending the importance of learning to speak the language of those who are being evange-

14. See Moreau's chapter in this volume on the importance of the creeds in Christian formation and the subsequent content the creeds supply to the initiation process.

15. There is a great deal of work in the area of epistemology to guide evangelists through the waters of modern and postmodern views of knowledge of God. Helpful in particular is the work of Margaret Archer, Andrew Collier, and Douglas Porpora, suggesting how "critical realism" can provide assistance to admitting God into rational debate (Archer et al., *Transcendence*, 1); at this point, the work of Andrew Root is also worthwhile, as he brings to bear the important accounts of God's active presence in the field of practical theology rather than remain captive to empirical and materialist accounts of reality only—as practical theology has tended to do; see Root, *Christopraxis*, 140–41.

16. Root, *Christopraxis*, 205–6. See also Colin Gunton's chapter in *Different Gospels* on the "Spirit as Lord" as an insightful critique of modernist theologies on the one hand and as a classical and orthodox account of the way the Trinity can put Christianity on a more hopeful view of freedom on the other.

17. In advocating evangelism as initiation into the kingdom of God, Abraham is aware of the need for evangelists to keep in mind the kind of language they appropriate to communicate the gospel. He notes how, even in the early church, John's Gospel utilizes the language of eternal life—rather than the kingdom of God—to announce what God has done in Christ. Naturally, one of the strengths of mature evangelists is the ability to speak the language of those they are seeking to evangelize. This step is crucial in any evangelistic endeavor, though the guarantees of success are never certain (Abraham, *Logic of Evangelism*, 194).

lized, and he is prescient in knowing the significance of cultivating persons in community. Where Brown goes off course, according to Abraham, is with understanding the costliness the gospel inaugurates with respect to commitment, both intellectually and morally, and the kind of *community* necessary to sustain that commitment over time.[18] Simply extending the boundaries of the church to include secular persons without entertaining the weight of what makes the Christian gospel and community unique does not work, for rather than building on the foundational principles of evangelism as initiation into the kingdom of God, we end up with the erosion of Christian community from within at the beginning—a kind of Trojan Horse, so to speak.[19] That is, rather than theocentric, we paradoxically become anthropocentric in our approach to evangelism, as without the substance of the gospel, there is really no internal restraint on what we can do or believe, breeding what other commentators of culture now call "Therapeutic, Moralistic, Deism" (TMD) and others "Sheilaism."[20] What is left are values pertaining to personal freedom and autonomy, authenticity and fulfillment, community and supportive relationships. In other words, the demands of the gospel as classically understood dissolve before we even arrive on the porch of repentance and enter the door of faith.[21]

18. Abraham, *Logic of Evangelism*, 194–96, 205.

19. Abraham, *Logic of Evangelism*, 198. See also Abraham's chapter "Trojan Horses from Paris" in his *Logic of Renewal*, where he brings to light the way both Alexander Schmemann and Gilbert Bilezikian do not adequately take the importance of initiation in the Christian life into account: Schmemann does not take into consideration how initiation and catechesis may give persons appropriate knowledge and understanding before entering into the liturgy of the church; Bilezikian does not raise the bar high enough for new converts and seekers permitting them to set their own agenda. Both Schmemann and Bilezikian give away, in their own ways, too much of the store, piling on too much or requiring too little (Abraham, *Logic of Evangelism*, 90–2).

20. The phrases "Moralistic, Therapeutic, Deism" (MTD) and "Sheilaism" capture, in negative fashion, a minimalist, if not consumerist, mindset with respect to the way modern persons—whether inside or outside the church—may understand religious faith and practice. In terms of Abraham's proposal of evangelism as initiation, we could see how the one (MTD) truncates the full orbed nature of the gospel, while the other (Sheilaism) crafts the gospel to individuals wants and desires. Both views are symptomatic of modernity's attempt to reduce the gospel to manageable pieces. Helpful commentaries on MTD are Smith, *Souls in Transition*, 154–56; Dean, *Almost Christian*, 3–22; and, of course, Robert Bellah and his associates who coined the term "Sheilaism" in their highly influential *Habits of the Heart*, 221–35.

21. The allusion here is to John Wesley's image of the house to describe the Christian life; see my chapter in this volume on "Evangelism as Initiation." Also: though Abraham does not cite Charles Taylor in *Logic of Evangelism*, there is room to consider how

Therefore, lest we miss Abraham's specific contentions about Brown's approach to evangelism, we will also miss Abraham's central concern with respect to modernity: the way it has deeply infected evangelism in the West, even to the point of going unnoticed.[22] The reasons for this lacuna are many but, as Abraham demonstrates, the fallout has been severe: since Schleiermacher, modern expressions of evangelism have simply lost sight of the internal logic and constraints of the gospel and become cut off from the resources that could bringing healing.[23] Indeed, the debris from modern forms of Fundamentalism and Evangelicalism are in plain view; though the noise from these solemn assemblies continues, whether as reactions against historical criticism or theories of evolution, or as promotions of health and prosperity and self-esteem, even as predictions of apocalypse in the Middle East. Sociologically, modern evangelism has drunk deeply from the wells of secular culture. The entrepreneurial spirit is alive and active, along with the cult of personality and commercial success.[24] The microwavable future has arrived, though no one seems to have noticed.[25]

Therefore, it is not unthinkable that the fads and fashions of modernity have become more prevalent with the rise of various kinds of means of communication (of which social media is the latest manifestation). The theological trends of a secularized church were also part of the Death of God movements in the 1960s. It is why the "secular church" would appear to be an oxymoron, but as the decade moved on, so did the secular idea. In South America, for example, among Roman Catholics, Liberation Theology developed, which was largely a hybrid between secular Marxist thought and the Bible. Actually, one could argue that Liberation Theology was predicated upon the New Testament concern with justice. This stance was surely

---

Abraham might utilize Taylor's work. In his book *Ethics of Authenticity*, for example, Taylor narrates how the modern self seeks to inscribe moral claims by appealing to notions of authenticity and autonomy, where objective descriptions of reality are discarded for more subjective frames of meaning, 21–23.

22. Abraham, *Logic of Evangelism*, 199.

23. Abraham, *Logic of Evangelism*, 199; see also Vickers, "Medicine of the Holy Spirit," where he writes about the healing, if not therapeutic, work of the Holy Spirit in the life of the church and individual. Acting in and through the canonical materials of the church, the Spirit can heal the divisions that beset the church as well as remind the church of the rich treasures that can connect the church to its true source of healing: God (Vickers, "Medicine of the Holy Spirit," 15–26).

24. For the promises and perils of the evangelist's personality to the work of evangelism, see Gehring, *Oxbridge Evangelist*.

25. Abraham, *Logic of Evangelism*, 200–1.

embraced by Leonardo Boff, who was on the Left of the political spectrum, but remained orthodox in his theological commitments. The problem with Liberation Theology was that it was more Marxist than Christian. Indeed, David Martin's study of the explosive success of Pentecostalism in South American demonstrates that, in mission and evangelism, Pentecostalism has outgunned liberation movements. Liberation Theology divided the Roman Catholic Church and left a wake of concern among leaders (though Pope Francis has clearly been influenced by it). Therefore, whatever our views of the inadequacies of Liberation Theology, we must understand how it has ultimately failed to provide a balanced theology with a broader vision of mission, never being able to fully escape the secular nature of its political program.[26]

It is why Abraham insists that evangelists need not fear modernity but also must take note of how they may deploy the resources of the gospel to specific situations. The role of apologetics is a case in point. To be sure, as Abraham indicates, there is a place for apologetics in evangelism. There is a place to address a wide variety of issues as ways to gain clarity and avoid confusion, indeed, to humbly recognize errors and mistakes in the past.[27] However, there are also dangers. Too often, for example, apologetics can become too abstract and fail to capture the mystery of the gospel. It can act as a "substitute for a deep personal encounter with the living God" and fail to give an account of the inner witness of the Holy Spirit.[28] We can place too much emphasis on our own rhetorical and intellectual prowess, neglecting how the best apologetic strategy may involve the actual Christian community on the one hand and the vital inner workings of the Spirit on the other.[29]

---

26. Abraham, *Logic of Evangelism*, 203.

27. Abraham, *Logic of Evangelism*, 206. The work of John Stackhouse Jr. is helpful here. Building on the apologetical approach of C. S. Lewis, Stackhouse argues that the church's ministry of apologetics must be humble in at least three respects: epistemologically, rhetorically, and spiritually. Apologetics simply cannot be a reactionary enterprise; instead, it needs to share and defend the good news in ways congruous with nature of salvation itself (Stackhouse, *Humble Apologetics*, 228). We can find strong affinities between Stackhouse's approach to apologetics and Abraham's proposals to evangelism in the days ahead.

28. Abraham, *Logic of Evangelism*, 206.

29. Abraham, *Logic of Evangelism*, 207. We may also remember Lesslie Newbigin's insight into this evangelistic and apologetic task: that the best apologetical defense of the gospel is the local, concrete assembly of believers; the congregation in mission supplies the key hermeneutic of the good news (Newbigin, *Gospel in a Pluralist Society*, 222). John

Modernity has led us down many different theological rabbit trails, but as we have come to realize, there *is* more in evangelists' arsenals than may have previously thought. The modern world may not appear as grim as we envisioned. Indeed, contrary to the early secularization thesis, which stated that religion in general and Christianity in particular would go away (Comte and Durkheim), what we see now is a world taming in religion, that there is in the human heart an ineradicable question for spiritual reality.[30] Religion is alive and well. For example, with the rise of militant forms of Islam and the continual explosion of Charismatic and Pentecostal movements around the globe—not to mention how secularism seeks to establish itself as an alternative worldview—the landscape is actually fertile with evangelistic opportunity. It is one of the reasons we need to remain confident but cautious with respect to modernity and its offspring.[31]

But the challenges to the ministry of evangelism are real. Abraham is fully aware of the negative aspects of modernity on culture, the so-called "acids of modernity." He is keenly cognizant of how irresponsible it is to proclaim the good news without knowing the basic narrative of the gospel, or to invite people to make a personal decision for Christ without catechesis.[32] In fact, to proceed in such a fashion is cruel and unworkable: cruel because it offers light and hope in the midst of darkness and then leaves persons to the wastelands of false religion; unworkable because it does not equip Christians to lay hold of the importance of God's rule in Christ; persons are simply left to the cravings of their own desires (Rom 1:24).[33] Evangelism, as Abraham has conceived of it, requires a robust theocentric vision of God's reign that does not become too preoccupied with the anthropocentric thrust of evangelism since the eighteenth century; it requires

---

Wesley's doctrine of the inner witness of the Holy Spirit is apt here as well.

30. Abraham, *Logic of Evangelism*, 201. See also, Comte, *Cours de philosophie*, and Durkheim, *Elementary Forms of Religious Life*.

31. Throughout the chapter, "Evangelism and Modernity," Abraham counsels caution. To be sure, he is quick to cite how the gospel is not like a car that we can redesign and sell at will to suit the buyer and how we cannot adjust the gospel to every wind of secular doctrine. Instead, there are certain convictions and sensibilities we foster to carry out the ministry of evangelism with integrity; there is work to do, even it as requires patience and persistence (Abraham, *Logic of Evangelism*, 203).

32. See Abraham, *Logic of Evangelism*, 207.

33. Abraham, *Logic of Evangelism*, 207.

a posture of anticipation to God's coming kingdom that results in having the mind of Christ, trusting in the power of the triune God.[34]

Abraham has challenged all of us to be wary of modernity but not afraid it. The church *can* live in confidence with what God is doing in the kingdom. We can tell the gospel story with boldness and bring the weight God's great love to those are seeking to live in the light of God's mercy as well as proclaim with Jesus, yet again, how the gates of hell will not prevail against his church and its mission, thus putting modernity its place (Matt 16:18). The ministry of evangelism can thrive and flourish. The kingdom will come.[35]

34. Abraham, *Logic of Evangelism*, 208.
35. Abraham, *Logic of Evangelism*, 95.

Chapter Thirteen

Evangelism in the Postmodern World of Science and Technology

John Wilson

Introduction

SINCE THE WRITING OF *The Logic of Evangelism*, the dialogue between religion and science has increased significantly. For example, Stephen J. Gould questions whether religion and science can pursue truth together and suggests they cannot as they occupy different *magisterial*, which he referred to as "non-overlapping *magisteria* (NOMA)."[1] I agree with Gould that science only asks questions of the material world whereas religion asks questions of ultimate human destiny, meaning, and purpose. Otherwise, religion capitulates to science or science capitulates to religion, which is not good for either discipline. Science can only find partial truth—truth associated entirely with the material and religion with the eternal. To understand humankind's quest for answers to questions of purpose and well-being, we must turn to religion. Religion and science in working together can provide a coherent worldview.

Rabbi Harold Kushner makes the case well. Kushner, quoting Carl Jung, states how in *Modern Man in Search of a Soul*: "About a third of my cases are suffering from no clinically definable neuroses, but from the senselessness and emptiness of their lives. This can be described as the

1. Gould, *Rock*, 5.

general neurosis of our time."[2] Victor Frankl makes a similar point. In *Man's Search for Meaning*, Frankl discusses the importance of meaning in life as a prisoner in Auschwitz and other German prison camps. Prisoners, when they could no longer find any meaning in living, turned their face to the wall and died.[3] Lack of meaningful existence makes life empty and fails to encourage progress. Something that exists in the human psyche beyond reason compels us forward—the human spirit, the drive to move on to something greater, despite the pain. Frankl, Jung, and Kushner agree: intentional, purposeful, joyful life requires meaning, a worldview which the epistemology of science and technology does not provide.

John Polkinghorne, an Anglican theologian, makes a similar case in terms of the promise of meaning. In technical language, Polkinghorne refers to epistemology and ontology together. He says that "thought coming from the bottom-up" regarding Jesus, moves from epistemology to ontology. Early Christian writings provide evidence of this inversion in terms of Christ's resurrection, when something happened to continue the story. The New Testament writers point to Easter as that "something," the validity of which rests in the appearance stories and the empty tomb.[4] The early church's experience of God through the Holy Spirit becomes the basis of this view—a claim which science and technology cannot make.

The implications for evangelism, then, are challenging, as the church in the twenty-first century seeks to present the kingdom of God in language that the postmodern world can grasp as the apostle Paul did in Athens (Acts 17:22). Paul stood in the midst of the Areopagus and said, "Men of Athens, I observe that you are very religious in all respects. For while I was passing through and examining the objects of your worship, I also found an altar with this inscription, 'TO AN UNKNOWN GOD.' What therefore you worship in ignorance, this I proclaim to you" (Acts 17:25).

Successful evangelism identifies with the premises of the culture and shows how they relate to Jesus' call to repent and turn to God and away from forces of wickedness. The church can provide both the questions and the answers—apologetics for evangelism in the postmodern world.

Undoubtedly, apologetics in the postmodern world of science challenges evangelism in the highly technical twenty-first century. Noting the

---

2. Kushner, *When All You've Ever Wanted*, 18.

3. Frankl, *Man's Search for Meaning*, quoted in Kushner, *When All You've Ever Wanted*, 18.

4. Polkinghorne and Beale, *Questions of Truth*, 20–22.

importance of the need for evangelism to reach people in contemporary times, Arthur R. Peacocke comments on Leslie Newbigin's *Foolishness to the Greeks*: "No one concerned with the future of the Christian faith, or indeed any other religion, can avoid facing up to the impact of science on faith. This encounter is identified by Newbigin as the crucial point at which the gospel is failing to have any impact on "Western men and women."[5] The church often stood resolutely intolerant of science—as when it refuted Galileo Galilei's heliocentric view of the universe and Charles Darwin's publication of the *Origin of Species*, missing the possibility of how such discoveries enrich the understanding of God in creation. Shutting out the theories of science when they appear to conflict with religious doctrine has not worked in the past and does not offer an appropriate approach for the future. Evangelism, therefore, must find the path of working with science without sacrificing doctrinal content and do so in ways that look at order, intelligence, and beauty.

Throughout his writings, Polkinghorne makes this point, noting how a theistic view sees God as the source of order, intelligibility, and beauty. In beauty, for example, we experience God's joy in creation. In moral law, we experience God's divine will and purpose.[6] Beauty, however, slips through the net. Without saying how and why, Polkinghorne argues that art and music move us out of our cultural context.[7] The laws of physics, on the other hand, assure us of order in the universe, as life-forces evolve with the intellectual capacity to develop the mathematics and tools for observation and the ability to interpret the findings—the Anthropic Principle. Here, beauty is more subtle and difficult to explain, just as it is difficult to explain the experience of the divine, a point science cannot elucidate.

Therefore, evangelists in the church face a challenge, but they should state the challenge science faces as well; that is, in lacking the means to identify the source and cause behind creation and to identify the observed purpose in creation as the universe evolved to complexity. Evangelists can describe the questions which science cannot answer and tell the story of why and by whom the universe came into creation—of the God who put in place physical means in a purpose driven creation. The role of evangelism is not to sacrifice doctrine to pacify the scientific community to win converts.

5. Peacocke, *Theology for a Scientific Age*, 1.

6. Polkinghorne, *Way the World*, 20–22.

7. Polkinghorne, *Way the World*, 20–22.

Science in the Postmodern World

But what about epistemology? Here, we need to addresses the role of science in the postmodern world and the shift in epistemology from the seventeenth century to the twenty-first century. In addition, we also need to address the rise of pluralism, the increased acceptance of science, the "conservative" Protestant reaction to science, the rapid increase in the importance of technology, and the emergence of religion and science in dialogue, beginning with Ian Barbour.

However, it is again John Polkinghorne who can assist us, as it is Polkinghorne who acknowledges how both theology and science encounter *unseen realities*, from the invisible reality of God to the invisible realities of life on earth—from quarks to gluons. Physicists, for example, believe in quarks and gluons as they make sense of unseen physical reality. Similarly, theologians believe in the Triune God because such belief clarifies spiritual experience.[8] Both religion and science examine unseen realities and can potentially agree on this. Both theology and physics examine the evidence critically and realistically, as the texts of both disciplines show. Therefore, the theologian can explain the faith of the religious person analogically with the same confidence of the physicist who has never seen a quark. Both rely on pointers: religious experience in the instance of the religious person and measurement in the instance of the physicist.

And yet, over the last three hundred years, a shift has occurred in Western culture, a shift from a politico-ecclesiastical society to the rise of a secular nation-state. From Sir Isaac Newton's *Principia* to Bernard Le Bovier de Fontenelle's *Plurality of Worlds*, we have seen the enormous changes wrought in science by René Descartes's primacy of reason in the determination of all that exist. We have seen basic shifts at all levels of human endeavor in philosophy and religion. John Locke, an empiricist familiar with Descartes's work, for example, published *The Reasonableness of Christianity*, which argued for Christianity as the most reasonable of religions. Locke asserted that experience, coupled with probability, enabled humans to make judgments regarding God, eclipsing mystery.[9]

In addition, David Hume pointed out the weakness in the empiricist's position. Locke and the empiricists argued for the validity of their conclusions from experience, but Hume noted that no one had ever reportedly

---

8. Welker, "Romantic Love," 134–36.

9. Gonzalez, *Christianity*, 2:189.

experienced both cause and effect, routing the empiricists' arguments. What the empiricists argued is that what we observe are the phenomena of the event or its attributes—but not the event itself.[10]

Other shifts were occurring as well. In 1776, Adam Smith published *Wealth of Nations* as the Industrial Revolution swept Europe. Science and its methods stood strongly at the center of this change, which led more and more to a world looking to science for answers and into the methods of scientific inquiry.

These shifts, however, have come with a price. Pope Benedict XVI, for example, in discussing the "De-Hellenization of Christianity," says that such modern understandings of reason depend on a fusion of Platonism (i.e., Cartesianism) with empiricism (i.e., materialism). This fusion has resulted in two principles. First, we only accept conclusions from the mathematical and empirical premises as scientific; we measure claims to truth through this method. Second, once we begin, we realize how this "method" of science excludes God and reduces Christianity to a small piece of its originally established character.[11] This creates a problem, as religion falls prey to the trap laid by science that religion is unscientific. More importantly, no requirement exists which forces any mode of inquiry to be solely scientific. To do so would greatly impair the paths other than science in search of truth.

Such are the consequences of science in modernity emerging out of the seventeenth century. Scientists accepted a religious dimension of life and believed the rational character of creation and the Creator, but only through scientific investigation.[12] The loss of religious authority following the Protestant Reformation and the scientific discoveries of the seventeenth century thus created the conditions leading to modern pluralism in Christian belief, provoking a profound epistemological shift.

As philosopher Taedes A. Smedes has argued, the modern Enlightenment's acknowledgement of science resulted in a radical change in the West. This change gave rise to the acceptance of science's methods for the direction of cultural thought and attitude. Science not only influenced the material worldview of reality but also shaped the culture's direct understanding of reality. Smedes notes Owen Chadwick's comments:

> Something happened to religious people, which affected their attitude to the world; I do not say for better or worse, for gain or for

10. Gonzalez, *Christianity*, 2:191–92.

11. Benedict XVI, "Apostolic Journey."

12. Polkinghorne, *One World*, 1–3.

loss; a change in attitude remotely comparable to the change when
Greek philosophy became available to the schoolmen, or to the
change when the Renaissance altered men's attitudes to humanity.

Smedes concludes that such changes meant that persons no longer had
an awareness of God's providence.[13] But attitudes can swing and persons
can begin to search elsewhere for meaning, realizing that science cannot
answer the deep questions of human destiny. Therefore, the dogmatisms of
both science and religion can confound and confuse the believer and non-
believer alike, resulting in conflict. An evangelistic opportunity emerges,
but not without more confusion and turmoil, especially on the Protestant
front. As Hava Tirosh-Samuelson explains, the conflict between religion
and science continues when Protestant theologians—like Karl Barth,
Paul Tillich, and Reinhold Niebuhr—depart from the position of William
Paley[14] and no longer include science in their theological work. Evangelicals, Fundamentalists, and Pentecostals also exacerbate the problem when
they feel challenged by the discoveries of science, such as evolution. Their
positions result in events such as the Scopes Trial in Tennessee. Later, the
Baptist Henry Morris emphasized the literal interpretation of Genesis and
demanded biology courses include "creation science." In the 1990s, the
Presbyterian law professor Phillip Johnson insisted school curriculum include Intelligent Design theory, and the Discovery Institute in Seattle promoted Intelligent Design. These moves contributed to the conflict between
religion and science.[15]

But more change was to come. Advances in knowledge, particularly
in science, precipitated more cognitive dissonance in some areas of the
church's interpretation of scripture. Conservative Protestants continued to
take dogmatic positions that often excluded the discoveries in science and
used the courts to pursue their positions in the religion and science conflict
(often unsuccessfully). Such positions discourage dialogue between religion and science and impair evangelism.

In 1969, the Internet also began to make headway, starting with
ARPANET's networking of four separate computers.[16] Martin Cooper of

13. Smedes, "Beyond Barbour," 242.

14. In 1802, William Paley, an Anglican clergyman, published *Natural Theology*,
which argued for God's existence and character from nature. His work is best known
for the argument comparing nature and God analogously to a watch and its watchmaker
(Paley, *Natural Theology*, 7–10).

15. Tirosh-Samuelson, "History," 452–53.

16. Leiner, "Internet."

Motorola made the first cell phone call on April 3rd, 1973, from midtown Manhattan to Bell Labs' New Jersey headquarters.[17] Three senior Texas Instruments managers decided in 1981 to form their own company—Compaq Computer Corporation.[18] These developments made significant impacts on Western culture in the twenty-first century and altered the relationship between science and religion yet again.

Today, people rely strongly on technology and use it extensively in the new forms of social media. These changes also affect the means and way the church may evangelize the culture, as well as the content of the gospel. Now, the church must engage in fresh approaches in order to gain the attention of individuals in a world radically changed from the impact of science and technology. These shifts, therefore, are not only crucial to understanding the ministry of evangelism but also to the ongoing way in which religion and science may interact. Here, Smedes points again to the work of Barbour to suggest a creative way forward:

Ian Barbour's landmark book *Issues in Science and Religion* can be regarded as the starting point for the science-and-religion dialogue as we know it today—a field where scholars from theology and the sciences attempt to define the relationship between science and a religious (in most cases a Christian) worldview.[19]

Barbour's four categories of dialogue are important at this point as they suggest a way forward and as a way to comprehend the stages the dialogue may take. First, *conflict* will come into play, as apparent irreconcilable positions come into contact. Second, *independence* will raise its head, as religion and science operate in separate domains. Third, *dialogue* will arise when both religion and science realize how they can both systematically explore the same subjects in parallel and through analogy. In this instance, science might see that its discoveries raise questions for religion. Fourth, in integration, religion and science work together to develop a metaphysical synthesis. Barbour supports such a *synthesis*, as it can surpass both natural theology and theology of nature and push for a *synthesis* of both religion and science.[20] In dialogue, science can direct religion to questions to which science does not respond, and religion can do the same and direct questions to science to which religion does not respond. Such response respects each

---

17. Seward, "First Mobile Phone."

18. "Compaq Computer."

19. Smedes, "Beyond Barbour," 235.

20. Bigliardi, "Barbour's Typologies," 502–3.

other's position and encourages movement towards a coherent worldview. Further, it preserves Gould's NOMA discussed earlier. Barbour's argument regarding dialogue gives a strong path forward to enable religion and science to provide a more comprehensive worldview that answers the questions emerging in this dialogue—questions which neither religion nor science alone can answer.

Yet, science and technology do not answer the important questions of why there is something here rather than nothing, and why we are discussing it—the "anthropic principle." Science, in marvelous fashion, uncovers the secrets of the material world and provides ever-increasing standards for living, but only religion can answer the deeper questions of meaning and invite others into the kingdom of God.

This is the argument University of Chicago theologian Langdon Gilkey gave in a series of lectures where he argued that the world has purpose, but only through an understanding of creation. Religious practice focuses on God and the evidence associated with God in order to discover "truth," whereas science studies only the material world. Consequently, as human beings, we cannot solely answer the questions of meaning in the context of materiality or modern science.[21] Here, Gilkey noted the dissonance between religion and science in how they examine and understand reality: religion, which relies on God's revelation, knows God as Creator; science does not claim any scientific knowledge for God, as the scientist examines the material and cannot answer questions of meaning of the material world. Meaning goes far deeper and requires a relationship with God. Without a relationship with God, we do not have meaning.

Evangelism in the Postmodern World

It is why the ministry of evangelism has promise and where Walter Brueggemann's approach to evangelism may assist the church, as well as complement Abraham's argument, in telling the story of God's new creation, as evangelism does not ignore intellectual concerns but rather makes truth claims in support of God's reign in Jesus Christ.[22] Indeed, the church cannot ignore such claims. It does not need to sacrifice the content of the gospel for the sake of mission, becoming "secular" in the process, and losing the distinctive character of Jesus Christ and the church. Yet, in a postmodern

21. Gilkey, *Maker*, 125–207.
22. Abraham, *Logic of Evangelism*, 140–63.

context, the church must still find credible ways of sharing the gospel with the wider world.

In his chapter on "Evangelism and Modernity" in *The Logic of Evangelism*, Abraham suggests two ways to approach evangelism in such a context. The first is a traditional approach, where we view evangelism in terms of a general or well-maintained machine, having all the answers in line with the questions.[23] The second, which he supports, sees evangelism as "open to the new consciousness, as well as being universal, and inclusive . . . vulnerable, creative, poetic, subtle, fertile, dynamic, insightful, humble, relative, original, intuitive, imaginative, *new*, sensitive, loving, honest, and pluralist . . . birthed in a fountain of fresh insights."[24] In the postmodern world of science, Abraham thinks that people will not respond to traditional evangelistic language. The successful evangelist will need to adapt his or her message accordingly without a failure of nerve.

Outside the West, for example, millions of people suffer from lack of proper nutrition, healthcare, and education. There is little concern for postmodernism or science, only a fight for survival. It is a world similar to Jesus' world, where change needs to occur, but where such change also needs the life-giving change only Christ can bring.

It is why we think that Walter Brueggemann's concept of *promise* can complement Abraham's notion of evangelism as initiation into God's kingdom and as the way the church can address the Gospel in a postmodern, scientific world. The biblical term *promise* works well in such a world where it is not always available in a scientific world. The notion of *promise*, of course, begins with Abraham in Genesis and ends with the church in Revelation. It is a term that offers hope to those who have ears to hear or, as Bruggemann notes, who are seeking meaning: to the female outsider of a dysfunctional family who hears the word as *possibility*, or to the tired "businessman" who hears the word as *departure*, or to the permanent member of the underclass who hears it as *entitlement*. Three persons, previously open only to despair, now open to transformation in the common remembrance of *promise* in the biblical narrative.[25] In all three instances, the church can share a message—a word—that can acknowledge or gesture toward the accomplishments of science and technology in terms of education, nutrition,

---

23. Abraham, *Logic of Evangelism*, 186–87.

24. Abraham, *Logic of Evangelism*, 186–87.

25. Brueggemann, *Biblical Perspectives*, 48–70.

and medicine and yet also address the human cry for meaning, without sacrificing content.

Unfortunately, misguided approaches to evangelism can lead people to make decisions for Christ that are not well reasoned, do not emerge from a change of heart, and can shy away from the struggles of postmodernity. Such decisions often do not stand the test of time, and the new Christian does not continue in the faith. On the other hand, evangelism grounded in the kingdom of God, as Abraham advocates and as Bruggemann suggests, presents the Gospel in all its fullness, especially through preaching and catechesis, inviting people into the faith. In doing so, it does not need to back away from the substance of Christian truth claims, and can offer the eschatological hope of both the present and future without avoiding the acknowledgement of modern science.

Conclusion

To be sure, science has significance for the ministry of evangelism, especially with respect to the way the church may oversimplify the message and present inadequate content. For example, evolution may offer evidence for God continually active in creation and may provide evidence of God's purposes in evolution, but the complexity of evolution does not always offer credible evidence of God. Despite its success, modern science—and evolution in particular—lacks the ability to answer questions of human destiny and meaning, questions that only religion explores. The opening for the ministry of evangelism in the postmodern world, therefore, is promising. As Anglican theologian Rodney Clapp articulates, the church does not need to capitulate to the demands of postmodernity; the church does not need the nation-state as an ally to preserve the content of the gospel. Rather, the church has the gospel and can offer the promises of that gospel in the power of the kingdom.[26]

---

26. Clapp, *Peculiar People*, 16–32.

Afterword

WILLIAM J. ABRAHAM

OUR BOOKS ARE LIKE children. They leave home; some of them make friends; some of them make enemies. It is a delight to welcome this fine set of interpretative essays that tackle the central claims I advanced in *The Logic of Evangelism*. It is hard to believe that this volume has stayed the course for as long as it has. I am delighted that it has played a humble role in helping folks come to terms with a vital ministry of the church, which becomes all the more important as we move more deeply into a post-Christian culture in Europe and North America. I will not here take up some of the incisive criticisms that are laid out; I will leave it to the reader to sort through how best to respond. This does not mean that I am diffident or that I do not take them seriously; on the contrary, they are fine grist for my intellectual mill. My plan is to locate this volume in the wider evolution of my scholarship and theological development. This will, hopefully, bring out just how demanding the study of evangelism truly is; it will also illuminate the pivotal role that work on this volume had on my intellectual journey to date.

The title is important but can readily be missed. To speak of the *logic* of evangelism locates the analysis and argument in my initial training in the analytic philosophy of religion. In that world, the term logic signaled an intense interest in how to analyze crucial concepts that we generally take for granted in our thinking. This is no mere exercise in developing definitions; it cuts below the surface of our discourse to uncover all sorts of insight and confusion. It also lays bare, albeit indirectly, how one might proceed by way of positive assertion and by relevant argument. Thus, work on the logic of explanation in history seeks to clarify the kind of explanations that show up in good historical investigation—and thereby signals how the wider grammar of argument is deployed. Hence, I see this work as being a contribution to analytic theology, even though that designation only arrived after this volume was published. I suspect few of my readers noticed this feature of the material simply because they have not been exposed to the mid-twentieth century developments in Anglo-American philosophy. This is not offered as a criticism; it is simply an important feature of how I work more generally.

In fact, when I came to Perkins to work on evangelism, I insisted (even before I came for interviews) that I be able to continue my work in philosophy of religion. This was not a way to keep intact my identity after a risky move into a new field in practical theology; it was because I had a hunch that the skills developed in analytic philosophy could be important in this arena. The results are not always easy to assimilate; there is, at times, for example, some equivocation on how I use the concept of initiation. There is a shift between seeing initiation as the whole network of practices, including proclamation and catechesis, and seeing it simply as the practices related to catechesis. This can be very confusing; if I were to do a rewrite, I would have to clean this up. Note, moreover, that this angle of vision does not mean that we are simply baptizing the current usage and status quo in evangelism, an objection often levelled against some analytic philosophy. On the contrary, it creates space for critical evaluation and for positive proposals for the future. In this respect, I have learned a lot from my former colleague, Schubert Ogden, who argued that practical theology should be understood as the critical assessment of the practices of the church. Conceptual work is crucial if we are to proceed with this vision of practical theology; it provides the first but not the last word.

Another way to connect this approach with the study of evangelism is to think of it as a field-encompassing field. The procedure is simple: take an area of investigation and then bring to bear on it a select body of data that throws light on the phenomena. Thus, in the study of evangelism, I have drawn not just on analytic philosophy but also on biblical exegesis, on psychological studies of conversion, on various themes in systematic theology, and on church history, looking especially at what happened in early Methodism and the evangelization of the Roman Empire. The goal is to develop a thick description of evangelism and, from there, move to constructive proposals about theory and practice for the future. The wingspan can become somewhat daunting, to be sure; however, the results, even while they are selective, are surely fruitful and illuminating. All along, one can draw, as I did, on my own experience of being evangelized by my local church and its agents; I was also keen to draw on my own limited experience of ministry in radically diverse cultures.

It was far from easy to take up the study of evangelism as a serious sub-discipline within theological studies. I had one colleague—a distinguished student of religion and former high-level administrator—who openly ridiculed what I was doing in a classroom down the hall from where I was teaching. Other academics initially said that evangelism could not be taught. Given the paucity of good material, this was an understandable objection; however, when this objection failed, they then said that everybody really taught evangelism. It is a great pleasure to find less of this kind of nonsense today, even though we still have a long way to go to in getting a fair hearing. Given that I would never have come to faith if my local church had failed to evangelize, I found much of the opposition comical. Given my hardy Irish and independent background, I was not in the least deterred.

In time, I was deeply surprised at the quiet revolution that years of studying and writing about evangelism produced in my own life. I had read the early periods of church history in the standard way, tracing, for example, the relation between faith and reason, and exploring the conventional institutional developments of ministry and theology. When I read that history from the angle of evangelism, I was drawn into the remarkable material on catechesis that was so crucial to spiritual survival in the Greco-Roman world. Within this I had to come to terms with a whole new vision of the creeds of the early church. These were not written to gain tenure in the local university; they were hammered out by those responsible for grounding folk in the faith for the first time. Once this was in place, I was propelled into rethinking the very nature of systematic theology—a field that now has come to front and center in my thinking and scholarship.

The substance of what has emerged is that before they get to systematic theology, students need a clear grasp of the Gospel and what it means to enter into the life of the kingdom of God. Thus, we need both proclamation and catechesis before we even tackle what needs to be done in systematic theology. I stand by my claim that the heart of the Gospel is the arrival of the kingdom of God in Jesus Christ through the working of the Holy Spirit. This is quite different from an attempt to develop some kind of overall summary of biblical theology. I leave aside whether this is even possible beyond, say, a narrative of creation, freedom, fall, and redemption. The issue here is strictly historical: what did Jesus and the early apostles actually identify as the Gospel? And I stand by my claim that the various dimensions of incorporation into the faith minimally involve the six elements I isolate and discuss. Without dealing with all of these, Christian discipleship will be handicapped from the outset. The crucial follow through is then to see systematic theology as university or higher-level, postbaptismal catechesis. This hit me especially clearly when I came to realize that the various loci of systematic theology (from God to eschatology) were best seen as derived from the themes given to the believer in the creeds at baptism. I am still working out the full implications of this discovery, but it was while studying evangelism that the issue first came to my attention.

Friends and critics both note that, in a way, this is a recasting of a premodern program. Immediately, many gasp in unbelief because it does not compute with either modern or now postmodern sensibilities. My response to this has been longwinded and deep. On the one hand, I have defended this move by arguing for a very robust place of divine revelation in our knowledge of God. On the other hand, I have worked on creating the new sub-discipline of the epistemology of theology, so that the whole range of questions raised by critics of the intelligibility and truth of the Christian faith can be articulated and resolved at the highest philosophical level. Because of these developments, I am not in the least intimidated by the arrival of postmodernity. Postmoderns are often disillusioned moderns; they share the epistemological assumptions of modernity but find them unconvincing. The only antidote is to do genuine epistemology of theology and tackle questions of truth and knowledge as these relate to theology from the bottom up. Moreover, I am no more drawn to getting in bed with postmoderns than I was with moderns; shotgun weddings with passing epistemological proposals invariably fail. The Gospel and the Faith of the church cannot be confined to the epistemological, political, or cultural regimes of any epoch. We need to keep our nerve and retrieve both for our day and generation.

So, my relation to modernity and postmodernity is complex. So too is my relationship to contemporary evangelicalism. I am happy to own this designation, but only on two conditions. First, the crucial pedigree in play takes us back to my conversion within Irish Methodism. Happily, my work beyond that done in evangelism has permitted me to pursue that world with some depth. Second, it is patently obvious that much of contemporary evangelicalism does not have the resources needed to carry the church through the great crises of culture and history. Some critics, of course, want to use this label as a weapon against me, not knowing the wider interests that I pursue. I find it comical that those who know of my work in evangelism know little or nothing of my work in philosophical and systematic theology; likewise, those who know the latter are often embarrassed that I have worked on such an awkward arena as evangelism. I leave it to posterity to sort out the various layers of my identity. One of my deepest challenges is to keep my curiosity within manageable boundaries. My goal has always been to follow wherever my instincts and the arguments lead me; and I have sought to hand over this liberal arts tradition of scholarship to my students across the years. I value this as the heartbeat of theology at Perkins School of Theology. I also value it as I come to terms with the fine set of essays assembled here by devoted editors who passionately believe in serious academic work as it relates to evangelism.

List of Contributors

William J. Abraham is the Albert Cook Outler Professor of Wesley Studies at Perkins School of Theology. His numerous publications include *The Logic of Evangelism*, *The Logic of Renewal*, and *Canon and Criterion*.

Vaughn W. Baker serves the Senior Pastor of Silver Creek United Methodist Church in Azle, Texas, and the author of *Evangelism and the Openness of God*. He has given lectures on open theism and missiology.

Paul L. Gavrilyuk is associate professor of historical theology in the department of theology at the University of St. Thomas in St. Paul, Minnesota. His most recent publication is *The Suffering of the Impassable God: The Dialectics of Patristic Thought*.

Michael J. Gehring is Senior Pastor of Main Street United Methodist Church in Kernersville, North Carolina, and Adjunct Professor of Pastoral Theology at Hood Theological Seminary. He is the author of *The Oxbridge Evangelist: Motivations, Practices, and Legacy of C. S. Lewis*.

Robert Hunt is the Director of Global Theological Education and the Director of the Center for Evangelism and Missional Church Studies at Perkins School of Theology.

Scott J. Jones is Bishop of the Texas Conference of The United Methodist Church and formerly the McCreless Associate Professor of Evangelism at Perkins School of Theology, SMU. He is the author of *The Evangelistic Love of God & Neighbor: A Theology of Witness & Discipleship*.

Andrew D. Kinsey is Senior Pastor of Grace United Methodist Church in Franklin, Indiana, and Adjunct Professor of Ministry at United Theological Seminary in Dayton, Ohio, and in the Lantz Center for Christian Vocations at the University of Indianapolis. He is the editor of *Notes from a Wayward Son: A Miscellany* and the Wipf & Stock *Wesleyan Doctrine Series*.

William B. Lawrence is former Dean and Professor of American Church History at Perkins School of Theology, SMU. He is the author of *Methodism in Recovery: Renewing History, Reclaiming History, and Restoring Health*.

Phil Meadows is Professor of Evangelization Studies at Asbury Theological Seminary in Wilmore, Kentucky. He is also a senior research fellow at Nazarene Theological College and the University of Manchester. He founded the Inspire Movement, an international network of Christians that devotes itself to the practices of renewal and discipleship in the Wesleyan spirit.

Elizabeth Moreau is an ordained elder in the UMC in the Texas Annual Conference. She is the author of *From Called to Sent*, an adult discipleship catechesis.

Kimberly D. Reisman is the Executive Director of World Methodist Evangelism and Adjunct Professor of Evangelism and Ministry at Asbury Theological Seminary in Wilmore, Kentucky, and United Theological Seminary in Dayton, Ohio.

Andrew G. Walker is Emeritus Professor of Theology and Education at King's College, London, and author of *Deep Church: The Third Schism and the Recovery of Christian Orthodoxy, Enemy Territory: The Christian Struggle for the Modern World*, and *Telling the Story: Gospel, Mission and Culture*.

Karin L. Wende received her PhD at the University of Manchester. She is a Senior Fellow in the Polycarp Fellowship.

John Wilson serves as a lecturer in the Sam Houston State University Department of Physics and as the Zone 13 Zone Councilor for the Society of Physics Students. He is a Senior Fellow in Polycarp.

Ray Zirkel is a missionary, professor, and a member of the Evangelical Methodist Church of Costa Rica. A graduate of Asbury Seminary, Ray is also a fellow of the Polycarp Community at SMU. Ray is currently working on his PhD in Missiology at UNISA. Ray and his wife Lidia have two daughters.

Bibliography

Abraham, William J. *The Art of Evangelism: Carefully Crafting Evangelism into the Local Church*. 1988. Reprint, Eugene, OR: Wipf & Stock, 2011.

———. "C. S. Lewis and the Conversion of the West." *Perspectives: A Journal of Reformed Thought* 10 (1993) 12–17.

———. *Canon and Criterion in Christian Theology*. Oxford: Oxford University Press, 1998.

———. "Canonical Theism: Thirty Theses." In *Canonical Theism: A Proposal for Theology and the Church*, edited by William J. Abraham, et al., 1–10. Grand Rapids: Eerdmans, 2008.

———. *The Coming Great Revival: Recovering the Full Evangelical Tradition*. San Francisco: Harper & Row, 1984.

———. *Crossing the Threshold of Divine Revelation*. Grand Rapids: Eerdmans, 2006.

———. *El Arte de la Evangeligizacion*. Barcelona: CLIE, 1993.

———. "Eschatology and Epistemology." In *The Oxford Handbook of Eschatology*, edited by Jerry L. Walls, 581–590. Oxford: Oxford University Press, 2008.

———. *The Logic of Evangelism*. Grand Rapids: Eerdmans, 1989.

———. *The Logic of Evangelism: A Significant Contribution to the Theory and Practice of Evangelism*. Hodder & Stoughton, 1989.

———. *The Logic of Renewal*. London: Holy Trinity Brompton/Society for Promotion of Christian Knowledge, 2003.

———. "Methodism, Mission, and the Market State." In *World Mission in the Wesleyan Spirit*, edited by Darrell L. Whiteman and Gerald H. Anderson, 74–80. Franklin: Seedbed, 2014.

———. "On Making Disciples of the Lord Jesus Christ." In *Marks of the Body of Christ*, edited by Carl E. Braatan and Robert W. Jensen, 150–66. Grand Rapids: Eerdmans, 1999.

———. *Wesley for Armchair Theologians*. Louisville: Westminster John Knox, 2005.

Alford, Deann. "As Goes Costa Rica, So Goes the World?" *EMQ* 39.3 (2003) 324–32.

Ambrose (of Milan). "On the Mysteries." In *Nicene and Post-Nicene Fathers, Second Series*, edited by Philip Schaff et al., 10:317–25. Peabody, MA: Hendrickson, 1996.

Archer, Margaret S., et al. *Transcendence: Critical Realism and God*. London: Routledge, 2004.

Arias, Mortimer. *Announcing the Reign of God: Evangelization and the Subversive Memory of Jesus*. Philadelphia: Fortress, 1984.

Athanasius (of Alexandria). *On the Incarnation*. London: D. Nutt, 1891.

Barbour, Ian G. *Issues in Science and Religion*. New York: Harper Torchbook, 1966.

Barna. "Is Evangelism Going Out of Style?" December 17, 2013. https://www.barna.com/research/is-evangelism-going-out-of-style.

Bellah, Robert. *Habits of the Heart: Individualism and Commitment in American Life.* Berkeley: University of California Press, 1985.

Benedict, Daniel T. *Come to the Waters: Baptism and our Ministry of Welcoming Seekers and Making Disciples.* Nashville: Discipleship Resources, 2003.

Benedict XVI. "Apostolic Journey of His Holiness Benedict XVI to München, Altötting and Reensburg (September 9–14, 2006). Meeting with the Representatives of Science." Lecture. Aula Magna of the University of Regensburg. 12 September 2006.

Berger, Peter. *The Sacred Canopy: Elements of a Sociological Theory of Religion.* New York: Doubleday, 1967.

Bigliardi, Stefano. "Barbour's Typologies and the Contemporary Debate on Islam and Science." *Zygon: Journal of Science & Religion* 47.3 (2012) 501–19.

Blumhofer, Edith L. *Aimee Semple McPherson: Everybody's Sister.* Grand Rapids: Eerdmans, 1993.

Brockman, David R., and Ruben L. F. Habito. *The Gospel among Religions: Christian Ministry, Theology, and Spirituality in a Global Society.* Maryknoll, NY: Orbis, 2010.

Brown, Fred. *Secular Evangelism.* London: SCM, 1970.

Brueggemann, Walter. *Biblical Perspectives on Evangelism.* Nashville: Abingdon, 1993.

Butterfield, Herbert. "England in the Eighteenth Century." In *A History of the Methodist Church in Great Britain,* edited by Rupert Davies and Gordon Rupp, 3–33. London: Epworth, 1965.

Chilcote, Paul, and Laceye Warner, eds. *The Study of Evangelism: Exploring a Missional Practice of the Church.* Grand Rapids: Eerdmans, 2008.

Chrysostom, John. *Baptismal Instructions.* Translated by Paul Harkins. Westminster: Paulist, 1963.

Church of England. *Mission-Shaped Church: Church Planting and Fresh Expressions of Church in a Changing Context.* London: Church House, 2004.

Church of England. "Renewal & Reform." https://www.churchofengland.org/about/renewal-reform.

Church of England. "Statistics for Mission 2015." London: Research & Statistics, 2016.

Clapp, Rodney. *A Peculiar People.* Downers Grove: InterVarsity, 1996.

Clark, Neville. "Initiation and Eschatology." In *Baptism, the New Testament, and the Church: Historical and Contemporary Studies in Honour of R. E. O. White,* edited by Stanley E. Porter and Anthony R. Cross, 337–349. Sheffield, UK: Sheffield Academic Press, 1999.

Collins, Kenneth, and John H. Tyson, eds. *Conversion in the Wesleyan Tradition.* Nashville: Abingdon, 2001.

"Compaq Computer Corporation History." International Directory of Company Histories 26. Farmington Hills, MI: St. James, 1999. http://www.fundinguniverse.com/company-histories/compaq-computer-corporation-history.

Comte, Auguste. *Cours de philosophie positive.* New York: Calvin Blanchard, 1858.

Cox, Harvey. *The Secular City: Secularization and Urbanization in Theological Perspective.* New York: MacMillan, 1965.

Cupitt, Don. *Ethics in the Last Days of Humanity.* Salem: Polebridge Press, 2016.

Cyril (of Jerusalem). *The Works of Saint Cyril of Jerusalem.* Translated by Leo P. McCauley and Anthony A. Stephenson. 2 vols. Washington DC: Catholic University of America Press, 1970.

Darwin, Charles. *The Origin of Species*. New York: Signet Classic, 2003.

Dawn, Marva. *Reaching Out Without Dumbing Down: A Theology of Worship for this Urgent Time*. Grand Rapids: Eerdmans, 1995.

Day, Juliette. *Baptism in Early Byzantine Palestine 325–451*. Cambridge: Grove, 1999.

———. *The Baptismal Liturgy of Jerusalem*. Aldershot: Ashgate, 2007.

Dean, Kendra Creasy. *Almost Christian: What the Faith of Our Teenagers Is Telling the American Church*. Oxford: Oxford University Press, 2010.

Donovan, Vincent J. *Christianity Rediscovered*. Maryknoll: Orbis, 1987.

Dream City Church. "Our Story." https://dreamcitychurch.us/about-us/our-history.

Durkheim, Emile. *The Elementary Forms of Religious Life*. London: Hollen Street, 1915.

Egginton, William. *In Defense of Religious Moderation*. New York: Columbia University Press, 2011.

Ferguson, Everett. *Baptism in the Early Church: History, Theology, and Liturgy in the First Five Centuries*. Grand Rapids: Eerdmans, 2009.

Field, Clive. "Assessing the Decade of Evangelism." *British Religion in Numbers*. 2 March 2011. http://www.brin.ac.uk/2011/assessing-the-decade-of-evangelism.

Finn, Thomas. *Early Christian Baptism and the Catechumenate*. 2 vols. Collegeville: Liturgical, 1992.

———. *From Death to Rebirth: Ritual and Conversion in Antiquity*. New York: Paulist, 1997.

Finney, John. *Finding Faith Today: How Does It Happen?* Evangelism Research Findings. London: Bible Society, 1996.

Fox, Eddie H., and George E. Morris. *Faith-Sharing: Dynamics of Christian Witnessing by Invitation*. Nashville: Discipleship Resources, 1996.

———. *Let the Redeemed of the Lord Say So*. Franklin: Providence House, 1999.

Francis, Leslie, and Carol Roberts. "Growth or Decline in the Church of England During the Decade of Evangelism." *Journal of Contemporary Religion* 24.1 (2009) 67–81.

Frankl, Viktor E. *Man's Search for Meaning*. New York: Washington Square, 1968.

Gallie, W. B. *Philosophy & Historical Understanding*. New York: Schocken, 1968.

Gavrilyuk, Paul L. *Histoire du Catéchuménat dans L'église Ancienne*. Paris: Les Éditions du Cerf, 2007.

Geertz, Clifford. *The Interpretation of Cultures: Selected Essays*. New York: Basic, 1973.

Gehring, Michael. *The Oxbridge Evangelist: Motivations, Practices, and Legacy of C.S. Lewis*. Eugene, OR: Cascade, 2017.

Ghanea, Nazila, ed. *The Challenge of Religious Discrimination at the Dawn of the New Millennium*. Leiden: Martinus Nijhoff, 2003.

Gilkey, Langdon. *Maker of Heaven and Earth*. Garden City: Anchor, 1965.

Gómez V., Jorge I. *El Crecimiento y La Deserción de la Iglesia Evangélica Costarricense*. San José, Costa Rica: Instituto Internacional de Evangelización a Fondo, 1996.

González, Justo L. *Jaun Wesley: Herenica Y Promesa*. Hato Rey: Seminario Evangelico, 1998.

———. *The Story of Christianity*. Vol. 2. New York: HarperCollins, 1984.

Gould, Stephen Jay. *Rock of Ages*. New York: Ballantine, 1999.

Graves, Dan. "Yale Founded to Fight Liberalism." Christianity.com. 28 April 2010. https://www.christianity.com/church/church-history/timeline/1701-1800/yale-founded-to-fight-liberalism-11630185.html.

Green, Bryan. *The Practice of Evangelism*. New York: Scribner's, 1952.

Green, Joel B. *The New Testament and Ethics: A Book-by-Book Survey*. Grand Rapids: Baker Academic, 2013.

Gunter, Stephen. "E. Stanley Jones Professors Of Evangelism." Foundation for Evangelism. https://foundationforevangelism.org/e-stanley-jones-professors-of-evangelism.

Gunter, Stephen, and Elaine Robinson, eds. *Considering the Great Commission: Evangelism and Mission in the Wesleyan Spirit*. Nashville: Abingdon, 2005.

Gunton, Colin. "The Spirit as Lord." In *Different Gospels*, edited by Andrew Walker, 74–85. London: SPCK, 1993.

Haney, Eleanor Humes. *The Great Commandment: A Theology of Resistance and Transformation*. Cleveland: Pilgrim, 1998.

Hartman, Lars. *Into the Name of the Lord Jesus: Baptism in the Early Church*. London: A. & C. Black, 1997.

Harvard GSAS Christian Community. "Shield and Veritas History." http://www.hcs.harvard.edu/~gsascf/shield-and-veritas-history.

Hauerwas, Stanley. *Hannah's Child: A Theologian's Memoir*. Grand Rapids: Eerdmans, 2010.

Hawkins, Greg L., et al. *Reveal*. Barrington: Willow Creek Resources, 2007.

Heath, Elaine A. *The Mystic Way of Evangelism*. Grand Rapids: Baker, 2008.

Heath, Elaine A., and Scott T. Kisker. *Longing for Spring: A New Vision for Wesleyan Community*. Eugene, OR: Cascade, 2010.

Heim, S. Mark. *Salvations: Truth and Difference in Religion*. Maryknoll: Orbis, 2006.

Hick, John, and Paul F. Knitter, eds. *The Myth of Christian Uniqueness: Toward a Pluralistic Theology of Religions*. Maryknoll: Orbis, 1987.

Hill, Joe. "The Preacher and the Slave." In *The Little Red Songbook*, 36. Reprint, 19th Edition. Oakland: PM Press, 2014.

Hindman, David, and Daniel T. Benedict Jr. "Come to the Waters: Catechumenal Ministry at the College of William & Mary." *Liturgy* 25.3 (2010) 49–58.

Hindmarsh, Bruce. *Spiritual Autobiography in Early Modern England*. Oxford: Oxford University Press, 2005.

Hodgson, Marshall G. S., and Rogers D. Spotswood. *The Venture of Islam: Conscience and History in a World Civilization*. Chicago: University of Chicago Press, 1974.

Hoekendijk, J. C. *The Church Inside Out*. Philadelphia: Westminster, 1966.

Hoge, Dean R., and Jacqueline E. Wenger. *Pastors in Transition: Why Clergy Leave Local Church Ministry*. Grand Rapids: Eerdmans, 2005.

Holland, Clifton. "Conela: Resumen Estadistico De La Iglesia Latina Global." PROLADES. 2010. http://prolades.com/conela/costarica-stats-2010-CONELA.pdf.

———. "Latin American Population & Religious Affiliation by Region and Country, 2011." PROLADES. 2011. http://prolades.com/dbases/latam%20statistics/latam_population_and_religious_affiliation_2011_regions_countries-prolades.pdf.

———. "Public Opinion Polls On Religious Affiliation In Costa Rica, 1983–2012." PROLADES. 12 October 2012. http://prolades.com/cra/regions/cam/cri/cri_polls_1983–2012.pdf.

———. "Table Of Estimated Size Of The Protestant Movement In Costa Rica, May 2001." PROLADES. 29 January 2002. http://prolades.com/cra/regions/cam/cri/cri-tbl.htm.

Hopkins, Gerald Manley. "God's Grandeur." In *Gerald Manley Hopkins, Poems and Prose*, edited by W. H. Gardner, 27. London: Penguin Classics, 1985.

Hunt, Robert A. *The Gospel among the Nations: A Documentary History of Inculturation*. Maryknoll: Orbis, 2010.

Iglesia Metodista de Costa Rica. "Iglesia Metodista de Costa Rica." https://iglesiametodistacr.com.

Iyadurai, Joshua. *Transformative Religious Experience: A Phenomenological Understanding of Religious Conversion.* Eugene, OR: Pickwick, 2015.

Jackson, Jack. *Offering Christ: John Wesley's Evangelistic Vision.* Nashville: Kingswood, 2017.

———. "A Wesleyan Theology of Evangelism as Proclamation." PhD diss., University of Manchester, 2009.

Jensen, Robin. *Baptismal Imagery in Early Christianity: Ritual, Visual, and Theological Dimensions.* Grand Rapid: Baker Academic, 2012.

———. *Living Water: Images, Symbols, and Settings of Early Christian Baptism.* Leiden: Brill, 2011.

Jones, Scott J. *The Evangelistic Love of God and Neighbor: A Theology of Witness and Discipleship.* Nashville: Abingdon, 2003.

———. *John Wesley's Conception and Use of Scripture.* Nashville: Kingswood, 1995.

Kelsey, David H. *The Uses of Scripture in Recent Theology.* Philadelphia: Fortress, 1975.

Kim, Dong Young. *Understanding Religious Conversion: The Case of Saint Augustine.* Eugene, OR: Pickwick, 2012.

Klaiber, Walter. *Call and Response: Biblical Foundations for a Theology of Evangelism* Nashville: Abingdon, 1997.

Knight, Henry, and F. Douglas Powe, eds. *Transforming Evangelism: The Wesleyan Way of Sharing Faith.* Nashville: Discipleship Resources, 2006.

Kreider, Alan. *The Change of Conversion and the Origins of Christendom.* Harrisburg: Trinity, 1999.

Kreider, Alan, and Eleanor Kreider. *Worship and Mission after Christendom.* Scottsdale: Herald, 2011.

Lehman, Chris. "Joel Olsteen Worships Himself." *Salon.* 1 May 2012. www.salon.com/2012/05/01/joel_osteen_worships_himself.

Leiner, Barry M., et al. "Brief History of the Internet." Internet Society. 1997. www.internetsociety.org/internet/what-internet/history-internet/brief-history-internet#Origins.

Lewis, C. S. *Narnia, Cambridge, and Joy, 1950–1963.* Vol. 3 of *The Collected Letters of C. S. Lewis,* edited by Walter Hooper. New York: HarperCollins, 2005.

Lewis, C. S. *Surprised by Joy: The Shape of My Early Life.* London: Harcourt, 1955.

Libresco, Leah. "Lessons on Evangelization from the Largest Parish in the United States." *America: The Jesuit Review.* 5 April 2017. www.americanmagazine.org/charlotte-megaparish.

LifeWay. "Churchgoers Believe in Sharing Faith, Most Never Do." 13 August 2012. https://lifewayresearch.com/2012/08/13/churchgoers-believe-in-sharing-faith-most-never-do.

Lilla, Mark. *The Once and Future Liberal: After Identity Politics.* New York: HarperCollins, 2017.

Lossky, Vladimir. *Mystical Theology of the Eastern Church.* Cambridge: James Clarke & Co., 2005.

Machamer, Peter. "Galileo Galilei." In *The Stanford Encyclopedia of Philosophy,* edited by Edward N. Zalta. 13 June 2013. http://plato.stanford.edu/archives/spr2014/entries/galileo.

Malony, H. Newton, and Samuel Southard. *Handbook of Religious Conversion.* Birmingham, AL: Religious Education Press, 1992.

Maow, Richard J. *Called to the Life of the Mind: Some Advice for Evangelical Scholars.* Grand Rapids: Eerdmans, 2014.

Markham, Paul. *Rewired: Exploring Religious Conversion.* Eugene, OR: Wipf and Stock, 2007.

Martin, David. *A General Theory of Secularization.* New York: Harper Colophon, 1978.

———. *Tongues of Fire: The Explosion of Protestantism in Latin America.* Cambridge: Blackwell, 1990.

Maslow, A. H. "A Theory of Human Motivation." *Psychological Review* 50.4 (1943) 370–96.

Mastronardi, Monica. "Discipleship: Being And Making Disciples." Didache Faithful Teaching. 9 January 2008. http://didache.nazarene.org/index.php/regiontheoconf/ ibero-amer-theo-conf/545-iberoamo4-eng-62-discipleship/file.

Masuzawa, Tomoko. *The Invention of World Religions, Or, How European Universalism Was Preserved in the Language of Pluralism.* Chicago: University of Chicago Press, 2005.

McIntosh, Steve. *The Presence of the Infinite: The Spiritual Experience of Beauty, Truth, and Goodness.* Wheaton, IL: Quest, 2015.

Methodist Church. "Bring one person to faith this year." 27 June 2015. https://www. methodist.org.uk/about-us/news/latest-news/all-news/bring-one-person-to-faith- this-year-methodist-president-urges-churches.

Methodist Church. "Statistics for Mission 2014." https://www.methodist.org.uk/ media/2932/conf-2014-37-statistics-for-mssion.pdf

Methodist Church. "Views of the Church." http://www.methodist.org.uk/who-we-are/ vision-values.

Morgenthaler, Sally. *Worship Evangelism: Inviting Unbelievers into the Presence of God.* Grand Rapids: Zondervan, 1998.

Newbigin, Lesslie. *The Gospel in a Pluralist Society.* Grand Rapids: Eerdmans, 1989.

Nussbaum, Martha C. *The New Religious Intolerance: Overcoming the Politics of Fear in an Anxious Age.* Cambridge: Belknap, 2012.

Ogden, Schubert M. *Is There Only One True Religion or Are There Many?* Dallas: Southern Methodist University Press, 1992.

Paley, William. *Natural Theology.* Oxford: Oxford University Press, 2006.

Park, John S. *Holiness as a Root of Morality: Essays on Wesleyan Ethics: Essays in Honor of Lane A. Scott.* Lewiston: Edwin Mellen, 2006.

Peacocke, Arthur. *Theology for a Scientific Age.* Minneapolis: Fortress, 1993.

Perkins School of Theology. "Perkins' Mission." SMU Perkins. 2 April 2001. http://www. smu.edu/Perkins/About/Mission.

Polkinghorne, John C. "The Metaphysics of Divine Action." In *Chaos and Complexity,* edited by Robert John Russell et al., 147–56. Vatican: Vatican Observatory, 2000.

———. *One World.* Princeton: Princeton University Press, 1987.

———. *The Way the World Is.* London: Triangle, 1994.

Polkinghorne, John C., and Nicholas Beale. *Questions of Truth.* Louisville: Westminster John Knox, 2009.

Porter, Stanley E., and Anthony R. Cross, eds. *Baptism, the New Testament, and the Church: Historical and Contemporary Studies in Honor of R. E. O. White.* Sheffield, UK: Sheffield Academic Press, 1999.

———. *Dimensions of Baptism: Biblical and Theological Studies*. London: Bloomsbury and T. & T. Clark, 2003.

Proeschold-Bell, Jean Rae, and Patrick J. McDevitt. "An Overview of the History and Current Status of Clergy Health." *Journal of Prevention & Intervention in the Community* 40.3 (2012) 177–79.

Proeschold-Bell, Jean Rae, and Sara H. LeGrand., "High Rates of Obesity and Chronic Disease among United Methodist Clergy." *Obesity* 18.9 (2010) 1867–70.

Reisman, Kimberly D. "Evangelism as Embrace of the Other." PhD diss., University of Durham, 2013.

Robinson, Elaine A. *Godbearing: Evangelism Reconceived*. Cleveland: Pilgrim, 2006.

Robinson, John A. T. *Honest to God*. Philadelphia: Westminster, 1963.

Root, Andrew. *Christopraxis: A Practical Theology of the Cross*. Minneapolis: Fortress, 2014.

Schleiermacher, Friedrich. *The Christian Faith*. Edinburgh: T. & T. Clark, 1999.

Schrag, Calvin O. *The Self after Postmodernity*. New Haven: Yale University Press, 1997.

Senn, Frank. *The Witness of the Worshipping Community: Liturgy and the Practice of Evangelism*. New York: Paulist, 1993.

Seward, Zachary M. "The First Mobile Phone Call Was Made 40 Years Ago Today." The Atlantic. 3 April 2013. http://www.theatlantic.com/technology/archive/2013/04/the-first-mobile-phone-call-was-made-40-years-ago-today/274611.

Slagle, Amy. *The Eastern Church in the Spiritual Marketplace: American Conversions to Orthodox Christianity*. DeKalb: Northern Illinois University Press, 2011.

Smedes, Taede A. "Beyond Barbour or Back to Basics? The Future of Science-and-Religion and the Quest for Unity." *Zygon* 43.1 (2008) 235–58.

Smith, Christian. *Souls in Transition: The Religious and Spiritual Lives of Emerging Adults*. Oxford: Oxford University Press, 2009.

Smith, Huston. *The World's Religions*. New York: HarperOne, 1991.

Smith, Wilfred Cantwell. *The Meaning and End of Religion: A New Approach to the Religious Traditions of Mankind*. New York: Macmillan, 1963.

Stackhouse, John Jr. *Humble Apologetics: Defending the Faith Today*. Oxford: Oxford University Press, 2002.

Stetzer, Ed. "If it doesn't stem its decline, mainline Protestantism has just 23 Easters left." *The Washington Post*. April 28, 2017. https://www.washingtonpost.com/news/acts-of-faith/wp/2017/04/28/if-it-doesnt-stem-its-decline-mainline-protestantism-has-just-23-easters-left.

Stone, Bryan. *Evangelism after Christendom: The Theology and Practice of Christian Witness*. Grand Rapids: Brazos, 2007.

Stone, Bryan. "Finding Faith Today project at Boston University." Boston University School of Theology. http://www.bu.edu/cpt/current-projects-2/fft.

Sweezey, George Edgar. *Effective Evangelism: The Greatest Work in the World*. New York: Harper Collins, 1976.

Swift, Art. "Honesty and Ethics Rating of Clergy Slides to New Low." Gallup. 16 December 2013. http://www.gallup.com/poll/166298/honesty-ethics-rating-clergy-slides-new-low.aspx.

Taylor, Charles. *The Ethics of Authenticity*. Cambridge: Harvard University Press, 1991.

———. *A Secular Age*. Cambridge: Harvard University Press, 2007.

Theodore (of Mopsuestia). *Commentary of Theodore of Mopsuestia on the Lord's Prayer and on the Sacraments of Baptism and the Eucharist*. Translated by Alphonse Mingana. Piscataway: Gorgias, 2009.

Tigert, Leanne McCall, and Maren C. Tirabassi, eds. *Transgendering Faith: Identity, Sexuality and Spirituality*. Cleveland: Pilgrim, 2004.

Tirosh-Samuelson, Hava. "History and the Future of Science and Religion." *Zygon* 45.2 (2010) 452–53.

Tolkien, J. R. R. *The Silmarillion*. New York: Random House, 1977.

Tracy, David. *Blessed Rage for Order: The New Pluralism in Theology*. Chicago: University of Chicago Press, 1996.

Tuttle, Robert. *The Story of Evangelism: A History of the Witness to the Gospel*. Nashville: Abingdon, 2006.

Van Buren, Paul. *The Secular Meaning of the Gospel*. New York: Macmillan, 1967.

Vickers, Jason E. "Medicine of the Holy Spirit: The Canonical Heritage of the Church." In *Canonical Theism: A Proposal for Church & Theology*, edited by William J. Abraham et al., 11–26. Grand Rapids: Eerdmans, 2008.

Vickers, Jason E. "To Know and Love God Truly." In *Immersed in the Life of God: The Healing Resources of the Christian Faith: Essays in Honor of William J. Abraham*, edited by Paul L. Gavrilyuk, et al., 1–20. Grand Rapids: Eerdmans, 2008.

Walker, Andrew. "Chuckling in The Shack." In *Notes from a Wayward Son*, edited by Andrew D. Kinsey, 288–92. Eugene, OR: Cascade, 2015.

———, ed. *Different Gospels: Christian Orthodoxy and Modern Theologies*. London: SPCK, 1993.

———. *Enemy Territory: The Struggle for the Modern World*. London: Hodder & Stoughton, 1987.

———. "Foreword." In William J. Abraham, *The Logic of Renewal*, ix–xii. London: SPCK, 2003.

———. *Telling the Story: Gospel, Mission and Culture*. 1996. Reprint, Eugene, OR: Wipf & Stock, 2004.

Walker, Andrew, and Robin Parry. *Deep Church Rising: The Third Schism and the Recovery of Christian Orthodoxy*. Eugene, OR: Cascade, 2014.

Warner, Laceye C. *Saving Women: Retrieving Evangelistic Theology and Practice*. Waco: Baylor University Press, 2007.

Watson, David Lowes. "The Church as Journalist: Evangelism in the Context of the Local Church in the United States." *International Review of Mission* 72.285 (1983) 57–74.

Webber, Robert. *Journey to Jesus: The Worship, Evangelism, and Nurture Mission of the Church*. Nashville: Abingdon, 2001.

Welker, Michael. "Romantic Love, Covenantal Love, Kenotic Love." In *The Work of Love*, edited by John Polkinghorne, 127–36. Grand Rapids: Eerdmans, 2001.

Wells, David. *God the Evangelist: How the Holy Spirit Brings Men and Women to Faith*. London: STL, 1997.

Wesley, John. *Explanatory Notes Upon the New Testament*. London: Epworth Press, 2000.

Whitehead, Alfred North. *Science and the Modern World*. New York: Free Press, 1967.

Whiteman, Darrell, and Gerald Anderson, eds. *World Mission in the Wesleyan Spirit*. Franklin: Providence House, 2009.

World Awake. "Interfaith Seminaries." http://www.awainterfaithclergy.org/?q=content/interfaith-seminaries.

Yeich, Brian. "Christian Perfection as a Vision for Evangelism." PhD diss., University of Manchester, 2014.

Zajonc, R. B. "Emotion and Facial Efference: A Theory Reclaimed." *Science* 228.4695 (1985) 15–21.